READING FOR TODAY 5
TOPICS
FIFTH EDITION

LORRAINE C. SMITH
AND
NANCY NICI MARE

English Language Institute
Queens College
The City University of New York

NATIONAL GEOGRAPHIC LEARNING | **CENGAGE Learning**

Australia • Brazil • Mexico • Singapore • United Kingdom • United States

NATIONAL GEOGRAPHIC LEARNING | CENGAGE Learning·

Reading for Today 5: Topics
Fifth Edition
Lorraine C. Smith and Nancy Nici Mare

Publisher: Sherrise Roehr

Executive Editor: Laura Le Dréan

Managing Editor: Jennifer Monaghan

Senior Development Editor:
Mary Whittemore

Editorial Assistant: Jennifer Williams-Rapa

Director of Global and U.S. Marketing:
Ian Martin

Product Marketing Manager: Dalia Bravo

Senior Director, Production:
Michael Burggren

Content Production Manager:
Mark Rzeszutek

Senior Print Buyer: Mary Beth Hennebury

Compositor: MPS Limited

Cover and Interior Design:
Brenda Carmichael

Cover Photo: The National Centre for the
Performing Arts, also known as The Egg,
Beijing, China.

ISBN-13: 978-1-305-58000-8

National Geographic Learning
20 Channel Center Street
Boston, MA 02210
USA

Cengage Learning is a leading provider of customized learning solutions with office locations around the globe, including Singapore, the United Kingdom, Australia, Mexico, Brazil, and Japan. Locate your local office at **international.cengage.com/region**

Cengage Learning products are represented in Canada by Nelson Education, Ltd.

Visit National Geographic Learning online at **ngl.cengage.com**

Visit our corporate website at **www.cengage.com**

Printed in the United States of America
Print Number: 02   Print Year: 2017

CONTENTS

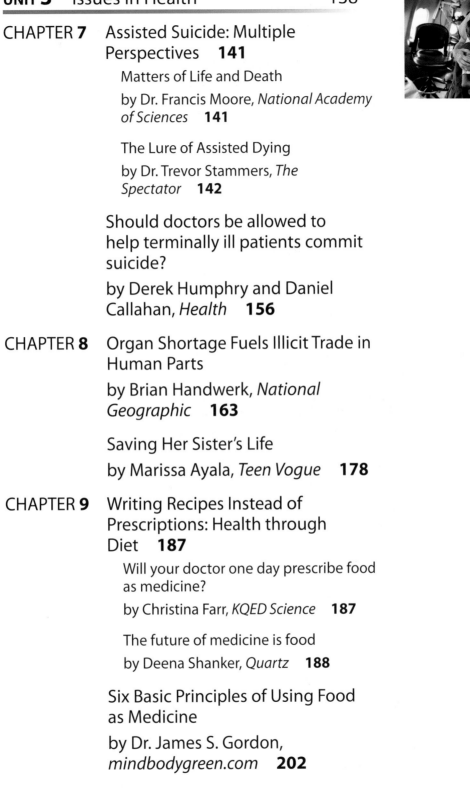

SCOPE & SEQUENCE

Unit & Theme	Chapter & Title	Reading Skills	Vocabulary Skills	Critical Thinking Skills
UNIT 1 **Trends in Society** Page 1	**CHAPTER 1** "Helicopter Parenting" Hysteria: Is it as widespread as we think? Page 5 Parental support during childhood is key to mental and physical health through adulthood Page 20	Previewing a reading Recalling information Scanning for information Summarizing information **Reading Skill Focus:** Understanding tables	Understanding meaning from context **Word Forms:** Recognizing the suffix -ment Understanding content-specific vocabulary: research	Supporting opinions with examples Comparing and contrasting different cultures Identifying types of parental support Determining the author's purpose
	CHAPTER 2 Retirement Home Meets Day Care at Providence Mount St. Vincent Page 27 College students are living rent-free in a Cleveland retirement home Page 41	Previewing a reading Recalling information Scanning for information Summarizing information **Reading Skill Focus:** Organizing information in a chart	Understanding meaning from context **Word Forms:** Recognizing the suffix -ment Using synonyms	Assessing viewpoints from quoted speech Evaluating the benefits of retirement communities Inferring information from different reading passages Assessing the author's bias.
	CHAPTER 3 Tablet Computers in School: Educational or Recreational? Page 49 Classroom Aid: Learning Scientific Concepts with iPads Page 65	Previewing a reading Recalling information Scanning for information Summarizing information **Reading Skill Focus:** Using headings to create an outline	Understanding meaning from context **Word Forms:** Recognizing the suffix -ness Understanding content-specific vocabulary: computer technology	Proposing ways that two different goals can be met Explaining opinions Assessing the reasons for adapting new technology Developing an opinion based on research Explaining the author's tone
UNIT 2 **Influences on Our Lives: Nature vs. Nurture** Page 72	**CHAPTER 4** What makes a child prodigy? Page 75 The Role of Families Page 76 How does insight help gifted children? Page 87	Previewing a reading Recalling information Scanning for information Summarizing information **Reading Skill Focus:** Organizing information in a chart	Understanding meaning from context **Word Forms:** Recognizing the suffix -al Understanding phrasal verbs	Explaining an opinion Speculating what might prevent child prodigies from being discovered Comparing research goals between studies Determining the author's viewpoint

SCOPE & SEQUENCE

Unit & Theme	Chapter & Title	Reading Skills	Vocabulary Skills	Critical Thinking Skills
	CHAPTER 5 Tragic Mistakes: When Children Are Switched as Babies Page 95 Damages Awarded to Families of Girls Swapped as Babies Page 96 El Salvador Babies Switched at Birth, Back with Parents Three Months Later Page 110	Previewing a reading Scanning for information Recalling information Summarizing information **Reading Skill Focus:** Creating a chain of events	Understanding meaning from context **Word Forms:** Recognizing the suffixes -ance and -ence Understanding content-specific vocabulary: *law*	Discussing the meaning of a statement Evaluating choices Assessing the reason for decisions Determining possible reasons for family members' actions Comparing the tone of different authors' writing
	CHAPTER 6 Who lives longer? Page 117 The Real Secrets to a Longer Life Page 130	Previewing a reading Scanning for information Recalling information Summarizing information **Reading Skill Focus:** Using headings to create a chart	Understanding meaning from context **Word Forms:** Recognizing the suffixes -ion and -tion Using synonyms	Analyzing the results of an experiment Discussing the reasons for longevity Comparing two sample groups Explaining differences in information between two readings Determining author's purpose
UNIT 3 **Issues in Health** Page 138	**CHAPTER 7** Assisted Suicide: Multiple Perspectives Page 141 The Lure of Assisted Dying Page 142 Should doctors be allowed to help terminally ill patients commit suicide? Page 156	Previewing a reading Scanning for information Recalling information Summarizing information **Reading Skill Focus:** Using a graphic organizer to compare viewpoints	Understanding meaning from context **Word Forms:** Recognizing word forms: verbs and nouns Understanding phrasal verbs	Speculating on rationales for doctors' actions Supporting personal viewpoint with reasons Evaluating pros and cons of assisted suicide Discussing a case study Assessing authors' perspectives on a controversial issue
	CHAPTER 8 Organ Shortage Fuels Illicit Trade in Human Parts Page 163 Saving Her Sister's Life Page 178	Previewing a reading Scanning for information Recalling information Summarizing information **Reading Skill Focus:** Understanding bar graphs and line graphs	Understanding meaning from context **Word Forms:** Recognizing word forms: nouns and verbs Using antonyms	Supporting opinions with reasons Comparing organ donation in different countries Explaining ideas about organ donation Inferring meaning of a statement Assessing the author's tone

SCOPE & SEQUENCE

Unit & Theme	Chapter & Title	Reading Skills	Vocabulary Skills	Critical Thinking Skills
	CHAPTER 9 Writing Recipes Instead of Prescriptions: Health through Diet Page 187 The future of medicine is food Page 188 Six Basic Principles of Using Food as Medicine Page 202	Previewing a reading Scanning for information Recalling information Summarizing information **Reading Skill Focus:** Using a graphic organizer to understand problems and solutions	Understanding meaning from context **Word Forms:** Recognizing word forms: verbs and nouns Using a Dictionary	Discussing ways that doctors might motivate patients to change their lifestyles Analyzing data and predicting trends Theorizing reasons for current programs and whether they may change Determining different authors' viewpoints
UNIT 4 **Our World and Beyond** Page 210	**CHAPTER 10** What is sustainable living? Page 213 A Model of Efficiency: NASA's Sustainability Base Page 229	Previewing a reading Scanning for information Recalling information Summarizing information **Reading Skill Focus:** Understanding bar graphs and pie charts	Understanding meaning from context **Word Forms:** Recognizing the suffixes -ion and -tion Understanding content-specific vocabulary: *environmental issues*	Assessing the benefits of sustainable living Predicting the consequences of not adopting a sustainable lifestyle Considering the challenges of sustainable living Drawing on one article to evaluate information in a second article Determining the author's purpose
	CHAPTER 11 Bringing Extinct Species Back to Life: Is it a good idea? Page 237 Extinction: Is it really that bad? Page 251	Previewing a reading Scanning for information Recalling information Summarizing information **Reading Skill Focus:** Understanding a graphic	Understanding meaning from context **Word Forms:** Recognizing the suffix -ity Using a dictionary	Analyzing the motives of others Discussing ways that extinctions of endangered species can be prevented Deciding what ethical issues are connected to bringing species back from extinction Explaining reasons for a writer's beliefs Establishing whether an author expresses bias
	CHAPTER 12 Life Beyond Earth: Almost within Reach Page 259 Hello? Anyone out there? Page 273	Previewing a reading Scanning for information Recalling information Summarizing information **Reading Skill Focus:** Organizing information in a chart	Understanding meaning from context **Word Forms:** Recognizing adjectives and nouns: -t becomes -ce Using antonyms	Speculating about other life in the universe Assessing the risks of making our presence on Earth known to any beings that exist beyond Earth Analyzing statements Inferring an author's opinion Determining the author's viewpoint

Topics for Today, Fifth Edition, is a reading skills text intended for advanced, college-bound students of English-as-a-second or foreign-language. The passages in this book are original articles drawn from a range of publications, thus allowing students the opportunity to read authentic materials from a wide variety of sources. As they engage with the materials in each chapter of this book, students develop the kinds of extensive and intensive reading skills they will need to achieve academic success in English.

Topics for Today, Fifth Edition, is one in a series of five reading skills texts. The complete series has been designed to meet the needs of students from the beginning to the advanced levels and includes the following:

- *Reading for Today 1: Themes for Today*   beginning
- *Reading for Today 2: Insights for Today*   high-beginning
- *Reading for Today 3: Issues for Today*   intermediate
- *Reading for Today 4: Concepts for Today*   high-intermediate
- *Reading for Today 5: Topics for Today*   advanced

Topics for Today, Fifth Edition, consists of four thematic units, each containing three chapters that deal with related subjects. Organizing the chapters into thematic units provides for a natural recycling of content-specific vocabulary and concepts, and discipline-specific sentence structure and rhetorical patterns. At the same time, each chapter is independent in content from the other chapters in that unit. This approach gives teachers and students the option of either completing all three chapters in a unit, in any order they wish, or choosing individual chapters as a focus in class.

Each chapter includes a second reading that relates to the topic of the main reading(s) and provides another perspective on the subject matter of that chapter. All of the chapters provide students with essential practice in the types of reading skills they will need in an academic environment. This requires students not only to read text, but also to examine information from various forms of charts, illustrations, and photographs. Furthermore, students are given the opportunity to speak and write about their own experiences, countries, and cultures in English and to compare these experiences and ideas with those of people from the United States and other countries.

The initial exercise preceding each reading helps activate the students' background knowledge of the topic and encourages the students to think about the ideas, facts, and vocabulary that will be presented in the passage. Discussing unit and chapter illustrations in class helps students visualize what they are going to read about and gives them cues for the new vocabulary they will encounter. The exercises and activities that follow the reading passage are intended to develop and improve reading proficiency, including the ability to learn new vocabulary from context and to develop comprehension of English sentence structure, as well as study skills such as outlining, creating charts, and understanding graphics, tables, and charts. The *Topics for Discussion and Writing* and *Critical Thinking* sections provide students the opportunity to master useful vocabulary encountered in the articles through discussion and group work and lead students to a comprehension of main ideas and specific information.

New to the Fifth Edition

Topics for Today, Fifth Edition, maintains the effective approach of the fourth edition with several major improvements. This enhanced edition takes a more in-depth approach to vocabulary development and application by consistently introducing, practicing, and assessing vocabulary in context while teaching valuable vocabulary-building skills that are recycled throughout the series.

The fifth edition of **Topics for Today** contains ten completely new chapters: *"Helicopter Parenting" Hysteria: Is it as widespread as we think?*, *Retirement Home Meets Day Care at Providence Mount St. Vincent*, and *Tablet Computers in School: Educational or Recreational?* in Unit 1, *What makes a child prodigy?* and *Tragic Mistakes: When Children Are Switched as Babies* in Unit 2, *Organ Shortage Fuels Illicit Trade in Human Parts* and *Writing Recipes Instead of Prescriptions: Health through Diet* in Unit 3, *What is sustainable living?*, *Bringing Extinct Species Back to Life: Is it a good idea?*, and *Life Beyond Earth: Almost within Reach* in Unit 4. In addition, the two original remaining chapters, *Who lives longer?* and *Assisted Suicide: Multiple Perspectives*, have been completely updated, and include new readings.

Several extensive changes have also been made throughout the text in the approaches to learning vocabulary and acquiring specific reading skills, and several new exercises have been added. The first is a new *Vocabulary Skills* section consisting of two parts. The first is a *Word Forms* exercise through which students practice vocabulary within the context of the readings. The second section emphasizes various vocabulary skills, for example, content-specific vocabulary, antonyms, synonyms, phrasal verbs, and dictionary skills. A third new exercise, *Vocabulary in Context*, gives students additional practice in language from the chapter in a new context. A new *Reading Skill* section focuses on a specific reading skill, for example, understanding graphics, charts, and tables, and creating outlines, charts, timelines, and chains of events. Also new to the fifth edition is an expanded *Critical Thinking* section, which includes questions about an author's purpose, tone, viewpoint, and/or bias. The activities in this section encourage students to use the information and vocabulary from the reading passages both orally and in writing, and to think beyond the reading passage and form their own opinions. In addition, the fifth edition includes new photos, graphs, and charts, all of which are designed to enhance students' comprehension of the readings. Finally, there is a crossword puzzle at the end of each chapter to reinforce vocabulary in the readings.

These revisions and enhancements to *Topics for Today, Fifth Edition,* have been designed to help students improve their reading skills and develop confidence as they work through the text. At the same time, the fifth edition is structured so that teachers can observe students steadily progressing toward skillful, independent reading.

How to Use This Book

Every chapter in this book consists of the following:

- *Prereading*
- *Reading*
- *Statement Evaluation*
- *Reading Analysis*
- *Vocabulary Skills*
- *Vocabulary in Context*
- *Reading Skill*
- *Information Recall*
- *Another Perspective*
- *Questions for Another Perspective*
- *Topics for Discussion and Writing*
- *Critical Thinking*
- *Crossword Puzzle*

The format of the chapters in the book is consistent. Although each chapter can be done entirely in class, some exercises may be assigned for homework. This, of course, depends on the individual teacher's preference, as well as the availability of class time.

Prereading

The prereading activity is designed to stimulate student interest and provide preliminary vocabulary for the passage itself. The importance of prereading should not be underestimated. Studies have shown the positive effect of prereading in motivating student interest, activating background knowledge, and enhancing reading comprehension. Time should be spent describing and discussing both unit and chapter photographs and illustrations as well as discussing the title and the prereading questions. Furthermore, the students should consider the source of the article, relate the topic to their own experiences, and predict what they are going to read.

Reading

Research has demonstrated the value of multiple readings, especially where each reading serves a specific purpose. The students will read each passage several times. As they read the passage(s) for the first time, they should be encouraged to read *ideas.* In English, ideas are in groups of words in sentences and in paragraphs, not in individual words. During subsequent readings, students will note headings, identify supporting details, look for inferences, and work on learning vocabulary from context.

Statement Evaluation

After the first reading, students will read the statements in the exercise, then go back to the passage and scan for the information that will clarify whether each is true or false, or whether it is an inference or not mentioned. If the statement is false, the students will rewrite the statement so that it becomes true. This activity can be done individually or in groups.

Reading Analysis

The students will read each question and answer it. This exercise deals with vocabulary from context, transition words, punctuation clues, sentence structure, sentence comprehension, and pronoun referents. The teacher should review personal and relative pronouns before doing this section. This exercise may be assigned for homework, or it may be done in class individually or in groups, giving the students the opportunity to discuss reasons for their answers.

Vocabulary Skills

This section consists of two parts. Part 1 focuses on recognizing word forms. As an introduction to this exercise, it is recommended that teachers first review parts of speech, especially verbs, nouns, adjectives, and adverbs. Teachers should point out the position of each word form in a sentence. Students will develop a sense for which part of speech is missing in a given sentence. Teachers should also point out clues to verb form and number, and whether an idea is affirmative or negative. Each section has its own instructions, depending on the particular pattern that is being introduced. For example, in the section containing words that take *-tion* in the noun form, teachers can explain that in the exercise students will look at the verb and noun forms of these words. Teachers can use the examples in the directions for each chapter's *Recognizing Word Forms* section to see that the students understand the exercise. All of the sentences in this exercise are content-specific, which helps not only reinforce the vocabulary, but also helps check the students' comprehension of the passage. This activity is very effective when done in pairs because students can discuss their answers. After students have a working knowledge of this type of exercise, it can be assigned for homework.

The focus of the new Part 2 of the *Vocabulary Skills* section varies. The purpose of this section is to provide students with a range of ways to learn and practice new vocabulary and make logical connections by working with words that are commonly paired or that are related to a particular topic. The exercises in this section focus on a variety of important vocabulary-related topics, such as content-specific vocabulary, antonyms, synonyms, phrasal verbs, and dictionary usage.

Vocabulary in Context

This is a fill-in exercise designed as a review of the vocabulary items covered in the *Reading Analysis* and/or the previous *Vocabulary Skills* exercises. In this exercise, the target words are used in new contexts, giving students the opportunity for additional practice. It can be assigned for homework as a review or done in class as group work.

Reading Skill

Each chapter includes a new *Reading Skill* section, which provides instruction and practice with a specific reading skill, such as understanding graphics, tables, pie charts, line graphs or bar graphs, or creating a chart, a chain of events, or an outline. This section is very effective when done in pairs or small groups. The exercises in these sections may also be done individually, but group work gives the students an opportunity to discuss their work.

Information Recall

This section requires students to review the passage again, in some cases along with the *Reading Skill* exercise, and answer questions that test the students' overall comprehension of the chapter. In addition, students must also write a short summary of the passage using no more than five sentences. In early chapters, the first sentence is given as a guide.

Another Perspective

The second reading in each chapter provides another point of view, or an additional topic, related to the main reading. The students should focus on general comprehension and on relating this reading to the primary reading.

Questions for Another Perspective

These questions are designed to check general comprehension of the second reading. They also provide the students with an opportunity to critically think about the topic of the chapter and formulate and express their opinions.

Topics for Discussion and Writing

This section provides ideas or questions for students to think about and work on alone, in pairs, or in small groups. Students are encouraged to use the information and vocabulary from the passages both orally and in their writing. The writing assignments may be done entirely in class, started in class and finished at home, or done entirely for homework. The last activity in this section is a journal-writing assignment that provides students with an opportunity to reflect on the topic of the chapter and respond to it in some personal way. Students should be encouraged to keep a journal and to write in it regularly. The students' journal writing may be purely personal, or students may choose to have the teacher read their entries. If the teacher reads the entries, the journals should be considered a free-writing activity and should be responded to rather than corrected.

Critical Thinking

This section contains various activities appropriate to the information in the passages. Some activities are designed for pair and small group work. Students are encouraged to use the information and vocabulary from the passages both orally and in writing. The critical thinking questions and activities provide students with an opportunity to think about some aspect of the chapter topic and to share their own thoughts and opinions about it. The goal of this section is for students to go beyond the reading itself and to form their own ideas and opinions on aspects of the topic. Additionally, students are asked to consider and discuss the author's purpose, tone, viewpoint, and/or bias. Teachers may also use these questions and activities as homework or in-class assignments. The activities in the *Critical Thinking* sections help students interact with the real world, as many exercises require students to go outside the classroom to collect specific information.

Crossword Puzzle

The *Crossword Puzzle* in each chapter is based on the vocabulary addressed in that chapter. Students can go over the puzzle orally if pronunciation practice with letters is needed. Teachers can have the students spell out their answers in addition to pronouncing the words themselves. Students invariably enjoy doing crossword puzzles. They are a fun way to reinforce the vocabulary presented in the various exercises in each chapter. Crossword puzzles also require students to pay attention to correct spelling. If the teacher prefers, students can do the *Crossword Puzzle* on their own or with a partner in their free time or after they have completed an in-class assignment and are waiting for the rest of their classmates to finish.

Index of Key Words and Phrases

The *Index of Key Words and Phrases* is at the back of the book. This section contains words and phrases from all the chapters for easy reference. This index can help students locate words they need or wish to review. The words that are part of the Academic Word List are indicated with an icon.

Skills Index

The Skills Index lists the different skills presented and/or practiced in the book.

ACKNOWLEDGMENTS

The authors and publisher would like to thank the following reviewers:

Sola Armanious, Hudson County Community College; **Marina Broeder**, Mission College; **Kara Chambers**, Mission College; **Peter Chin**, Waseda University International; **Feri Collins**, BIR Training Center; **Courtney DeRouen**, University of Washington; **Jeanne de Simon**, University of West Florida; **Shoshana Dworkin**, BIR Training Center; **Cindy Etter**, University of Washington International and English Language Programs; **Ken Fackler**, University of Tennessee at Martin; **Jan Hinson**, Carson Newman University; **Chigusa Katoku**, Mission College; **Sharon Kruzic**, Mission College; **Carmella Lieskle**, Shimane University; **Yelena Malchenko**, BIR Training Center; **Mercedes Mont**, Miami Dade College; **Ewa Paluch**, BIR Training Center; **Barbara Pijan**, Portland State University, Intensive English Language Program; **Julaine Rosner**, Mission College; **Julie Scales**, University of Washington; **Mike Sfiropoulos**, Palm Beach State College; **Barbara Smith-Palinkas**, Hillsborough Community College; **Eileen Sotak**, BIR Training Center; **Matthew Watterson**, Hongik University; **Tristinn Williams**, IELP—University of Washington; **Iryna Zhylina**, Hudson County Community College; **Ana Zuljevic**, BIR Training Center

Acknowledgments from Authors
We are thankful to everyone at Cengage, especially Laura LeDréan, Mary Whittemore, Patricia Giunta, Lori Solbakken, and Jennifer Williams-Rapa for their unwavering support. We are extremely grateful to all the teachers and students who use our book and who never hesitate to give us such incredible feedback. As always, we are very appreciative of the ongoing encouragement from our families, friends, and colleagues.

L.C.S. and N.N.M.

Dedication:

To our parents: Peg and Smitty; Anthony and Antoinette

Trends in Society

1. Are your parents very involved in your life? How much do you depend on your parents to help you make decisions?

2. Do most elderly people have a lot of contact with children? Do you think this is important? Why or why not?

3. Do you think it is important for teachers and children to use computers in the classroom? Why or why not?

3

Prereading

1. Look at the two photos.
   a. What is the parent doing in the first photo?
   b. What are the parents doing in the second photo?
   c. What might be the difference between the parent in the first photo and the parents in the second photo? Why do you think so?

2. What is "helicopter parenting"?

3. Read the title of the article. Do most people think that helicopter parenting is very common? Does the author think it's very common?

Reading

🎧 **Read the passage carefully. Then complete the exercises that follow.**

CD 1
TR 2

"Helicopter Parenting" Hysteria: Is it as widespread as we think?

by Alfie Kohn, *alfiekohn.org*

Parents who are overly involved in the lives of their college-age children are the folks we love to scorn. A steady stream of articles and blog posts bristle with indignation over dads who phone the dean about a trivial problem or moms who know more than we think they should about junior's love life. But it may be a good
5   time to ask just how common such incidents really are—and whether "helicopter parenting" (HP), when it does occur, is as damaging as we've been led to believe.

When you track down hard data, the results contrast sharply with the conventional wisdom. Yes, most parents are in touch with their college-age kids on a regular basis. But communicating isn't the same thing as intervening on a child's behalf, and the
10 latter seems to be fairly rare. The National Survey of Student Engagement (NSSE), which reached out to more than 9,000 students at 24 colleges and universities, found that only 13 percent of college freshmen and 8 percent of seniors said a parent had frequently intervened to help them solve problems.

As one university administrator told the *Chronicle of Higher Education*, "The
15 popular image of modern parents as high-strung nuisances who torment college administrators doesn't match reality." In any case, the students themselves certainly don't seem to be tormented by their parents. An overwhelming majority of the 10,000-plus University of California students contacted in a separate survey said their parents weren't involved in their choice of courses or their major.

20 Alarming media reports have also claimed that parents hover once their young-adult children enter the workplace, but there's little basis for that claim either. Michigan State University researchers discovered that 77 percent of the 725 employers they surveyed "hardly ever witnessed a parent while hiring a college senior." As for grown children outside of college and the workplace, the only study on the topic I
25 could find, published in 2012, reported that just one in five or six parents seemed to be intensely involved in their children's lives.

But what about the effects of such parenting on individual young people when it does occur? Here, too, a look at empirical findings yields surprising conclusions. For starters, some research has actually made a case in favor of parents' being very
30 actively connected—and, yes, even involved—with their young-adult children. That NSSE survey, for example, didn't find a lot of HP going on, but where it was taking

place, such students actually reported "higher levels of [academic] engagement and more frequent use of deep learning activities." Jillian Kinzie, a researcher involved with that project, confessed that when she saw those results, her first reaction was,
35   "This can't be right. We have to go back and look at this again." But the benefits did indeed prove impressive. As the survey's director, George Kuh, told a reporter, "Compared with their counterparts, children of helicopter parents were more satisfied with every aspect of their college experience, gained more in such areas as writing and critical thinking, and were more likely to talk with faculty and peers about
40   substantive topics."

     Meanwhile, in the 2012 study of grown children, "frequent parental involvement, including a wide range of support, was associated with better well-being for young adults." Support (not limited to money) from one's parents may be helpful, if not critical, when students graduate with uncertain employment prospects and,
45   perhaps, a crushing load of debt. A fair-minded appraisal of the subject suggests that denunciations of HP are based less on evidence than on a disparaging attitude about young people or on the value judgment that kids *ought* to become independent as soon as possible. That judgment may seem like common sense, but maturity isn't the same as self-sufficiency. Most developmental psychologists have concluded that the
50   quality of parent-child relationships continues to matter even past childhood. Good parenting is less about pushing one's offspring to be independent at a certain age than being responsive to what a particular child needs.

     But doesn't research show that HP can be psychologically damaging at least to some young people? A handful of small studies have shown that extreme versions
55   of HP sometimes go hand-in-hand with anxiety or a diminished sense of well-being. In each of these studies, however, questionnaires were given to students only at a single college, and the strength of the results weren't particularly impressive. Look closer, in fact, and you'll find two caveats to all of this research that are even more damning. First, the findings offer no support for the conclusion that HP *caused* the
60   problems with which it was associated. One set of researchers admitted that "when parents perceive their child as depressed, they may be more likely to 'hover.'" Those in another study acknowledged that unhappy students "may view their parents as more intrusive." Here, in other words, we have two alternative, perfectly plausible explanations for the (weak) correlation. One: if the parents are hovering,
65   it's because the kids already have issues. Two: students who are struggling may be more likely than their peers to interpret whatever their parents are doing as excessive involvement. Either way, the evidence doesn't prove that HP *makes* kids unhappy.

     The second major caveat is truly intriguing; its implications extend to the heart of what's meant by "overparenting" of children of all ages. When you read the research
70   closely, it turns out that what's classified as over-, intrusive, or helicopter parenting might more accurately be described as excessive *control* of children. This offers a very different lens through which to view all those warnings that parents do too much for

their children and are overly involved in their lives. If the problem is actually control rather than indulgence, we're forced to rethink the "coddled kids" narrative offered by most critics of HP, a narrative that fits with current claims that frustration and failure are good for children, that they have things too easy and need to develop more grit and self-discipline.

The ideal alternative, according to a growing body of research that I've written about elsewhere, isn't less parenting but better parenting. It's not standing back and letting kids struggle, then kicking them out of the nest and demanding they make it on their own whenever we (or pop-culture scolds) say so. It's being responsive to what the child needs. That may be the right to make decisions. It may also be a continued close connection to Mom and Dad. What seems clear about HP in particular is that it's neither as pervasive nor as damaging as is commonly assumed.

Statement Evaluation

Read the passage again. Then read the following statements. Indicate whether each statement is True (T), False (F), or Not Mentioned (NM). If a statement is false, rewrite it so that it is true. Then go back to the passage and find the information that supports your answers.

1. __T__ The results of a recent survey show that few parents of college freshmen actually intervene when their children have problems.

_____

2. __F__ Most college students want their parents to help them when they have problems.

_____

3. __T__ Helicopter parenting is a common occurrence.

_____

4. _____ In a survey at the University of California, a majority of students stated that their parents do not try to influence them in their course of study.

_____

5. __T__ In the NSSE survey, college students whose parents are involved with them reported that they are very engaged in their academic work.

_____

6. __F__ Children of helicopter parents do not do as well academically as other college students.

_____

7. __F__ Most developmental psychologists believe that the adult children of helicopter parents are much happier than other adult children.

_____

8. __F__ Frustration and failure are not good experiences for children.

_____

9. __F__ Most parents want their adult children to leave home and go out on their own.

_____

10. ____ Helicopter parenting may not be as common or as damaging as many people think.

_____

Reading Analysis

Read each question carefully. Circle the letter or number of the correct answer, or write your answer in the space provided.

1. Read lines 1–4.
  a. **Involved in** means
    1. thoughtful of.
    2. happy about.
    3. engaged with.
  b. **Scorn** means
    1. admire.
    2. ridicule.
    3. imitate.
  c. The first sentence means that
    1. we approve of parents who are overly involved in their college-age children's lives.
    2. we disapprove of parents who are overly involved in their college-age children's lives.
  d. **Indignation** means
    1. displeasure.
    2. confusion.
    3. sympathy.
  e. **Trivial** means
    1. ongoing.
    2. educational.
    3. unimportant.

2. Read line 5. **Incidents** means
  a. events.
  b. complaints.
  c. calls.

3. Read lines 7–8.

    a. **Track down** means

       1. research.

       2. locate.

       3. ask about.

    b. **Contrast** means

       1. confuse.

       2. agree.

       3. differ.

    c. **Conventional wisdom** refers to

       1. a generally accepted belief.

       2. a cultural tradition.

       3. a medical conclusion.

4. Read lines 9–10.

    a. **Intervening** means

       1. speaking.

       2. reacting.

       3. interfering.

    b. **Latter** refers to

       1. the first in a series of two.

       2. the second in a series of two.

    c. In this sentence, **the latter** refers to

       1. communicating with a college-age child.

       2. intervening on a college-age child's behalf.

5. Read lines 14–16.

    a. **High-strung** means

       1. confused.

       2. nervous.

       3. angry.

    b. Parents who are **nuisances** are

       1. popular.

       2. worried.

       3. annoying.

    c. **Torment** means

       1. bother.

       2. criticize.

       3. visit.

6. Read lines 20–21.
   a. **Alarming** means
      1. recent.
      2. disturbing.
      3. complex.
   b. **Claim** means
      1. tell.
      2. prove.
      3. state.
   c. **Hover** means
      1. watch over closely.
      2. listen to carefully.
      3. stay interested in.

7. Read lines 29–33.
   a. **Young-adult** children are
      1. between 13 and 19 years old.
      2. about 18–23 years old.
      3. college students.
   b. In the sentence, **engagement** means
      1. success.
      2. appointment.
      3. commitment.

8. Read lines 33–40.
   a. When Jillian Kinzie saw the results of the NSSE survey,
      1. she did not believe the results were correct.
      2. she believed the results were correct.
   b. **Impressive** means
      1. correct.
      2. remarkable.
      3. beneficial.
   c. **Counterparts** refers to
      1. other college students who are also children of helicopter parents.
      2. other college students who are not children of helicopter parents.
   d. **Peers** are
      1. your equals.
      2. your parents.
      3. your tutors.

9. Read lines 45–48.

   a. **Denunciations** means

      1. studies.

      (2.) criticisms.

      3. appraisals.

   b. **Disparaging** means

      1. narrow-minded.

      2. unsympathetic.

      • 3. very negative.

10. Read lines 54–55. **Diminished** means

     (a.) lowered.

     b. worried.

     c. sickened.

11. Read lines 57–61.

   a. **Caveat** means

      1. strength.

      (2.) caution.

      3. results.

   b. **Perceive** means

      1. view.

      2. misunderstand.

      (3.) know.

12. Read lines 63–67.

   a. **Plausible** means

      1. proven.

      2. true.

      (3.) reasonable.

   b. The two explanations in these sentences

      1. have been proven through research.

      (2.) have not been proven through research.

13. Read lines 69–77.

   a. **Indulgence** means

      (1.) allowing someone to do whatever he wants.

      2. controlling a person.

      3. giving a person a good education.

   b. **Coddled** kids are

      1. educated.

      2. cared for.

      (3.) spoiled.

    c. According to these sentences, helicopter parenting actually means
        1. caring about children.
        2. overly controlling children.
        3. helping children.

14. Read lines 83–84. **Pervasive** means
        a. negative.
        b. extensive.
        c. harmful.

15. What is the main idea of the passage?
        a. Helicopter parenting has been researched and found to be a serious problem that needs to be addressed.
        b. Helicopter parenting has been researched among college students, and the results indicate that it is not as serious a problem as many people believe.
        c. Helicopter parenting has been researched, but many more studies need to be conducted on this subject.

Vocabulary Skills

PART 1

Recognizing Word Forms

In English, there are several ways that verbs change to nouns. Some verbs become nouns by adding the suffix -ment, for example, involve (v.), involvement (n.). There may be spelling changes as well.

Complete each sentence with the correct word form on the left. Use the correct form of the verb in either the affirmative or the negative. All the nouns are singular.

acknowledge (v.)

acknowledgment (n.)

1. The _____ that frequent parental involvement was associated with a young adult's greater sense of well-being occurred after the researchers _____ the importance of parental support.

diminish (v.)

diminishment (n.)

2. A large amount of research has shown that helicopter parenting is limited. These findings _Diminish_ the belief that helicopter parenting is widespread. This often leads to the _diminishment_ of the important role of parents of young adults.

disparage (v.)

disparagement (n.)

3. Critics often _disparage_ parents who are overly involved in the lives of their college-age children. As a result of this widespread _disparagement_, helicopter parenting is often thought of as damaging.

engage (v.)

engagement (n.)

4. Students who were actively connected to their parents had higher levels of academic _engagement_ than students who _engage_ with their parents as much.

judge (v.)

judgment (n.)

5. Denunciations of HP are often based on the _judgment_ that all children should be independent as soon as possible. However, most parents _judge_ their children in the same way. In fact, they may evaluate their children very differently.

PART 2

Content-Specific Vocabulary

Content-specific vocabulary is very useful in understanding a particular topic, such as research. For example, it is important to understand the meaning of such words as *data* and *results*.

First, match each word or phrase with the correct meaning. Then complete each sentence with the correct word or phrase. Use each word or phrase only once.

f	1. associated with	a.	back up with information
h	2. body of research	b.	confirm as correct
g	3. cause	c.	data; facts
i	4. conclusion	d.	give an account of
e	5. correlation	e.	interconnection
j	6. empirical findings	f.	linked with
c	7. evidence	g.	make happen
b	8. prove	h.	number of studies on the same subject
d	9. report	i.	deduction
a	10. support	j.	results based on an experiment

1. The psychologist will accurately _____support_____ what he discovers when he interviews the patient.

2. The researcher has found a(n) _____correlation_____ between the child's dependence on his parents and his anxiety, but she has not clearly established the connection yet.

3. The NSSE continues to study college students' academic performance in order to _____prove_____ the importance of parental involvement.

4. Researchers need more _____evidence_____ to determine if helicopter parenting is damaging.

5. The most recent studies _____support_____ the active connection between parents and their college-age children.

6. The author of this article has come to the _____conclusion_____ that better parenting is more beneficial than less parenting.

7. There is quite a large _____report_____ on the subject of parent/child relationships. This topic has been studied for many years.

8. Studies have shown that extreme versions of HP are often _____cause_____ a college student's anxiety and diminished sense of well-being.

9. HP and other negative parental behaviors often _____ some students' emotional problems.

10. The _____ based on considerable research have shown that HP often results in students' more frequent use of deep learning activities.

Vocabulary in Context

counterparts *(n.)*	indignation *(n.)*	pervasive *(adj.)*	tormented *(v.)*
hover *(v.)*	latter *(n.)*	plausible *(adj.)*	trivial *(adj.)*
impressive *(adj.)*	perceive *(v.)*		

Read the following sentences. Complete each sentence with the correct word from the box. Use each word or phrase only once.

1. Hiro's English proficiency is _____. He speaks the language extremely well after only having studied it for six months.

2. Texting while driving was so _____ in this city that the government had to ban the use of cell phones by drivers.

3. Lori offered me chicken or pasta at the party. I chose the _____ because I'm a vegetarian.

4. We wanted to eat lunch in the park, but the mosquitoes __tormented__ us, so we ate in the classroom instead.

5. The student's excuse for not doing her homework was _____, but the teacher refused to believe it.

6. Our dogs always __hover__ near the table when we are eating, hoping for a scrap of our dinner.

7. The actor insisted on wearing a belt, even though this was a very __Impressive__ detail of his costume.

8. Although Yoshi's classmates _____ her as being very shy, she's actually very friendly and outgoing.

9. Professor Lee's students seem to have a lot more homework than their _____ in Professor Kim's class.

10. The president's __indignation__ at the reporter's question was evident from her sharp tone and loud voice.

Reading Skill

Understanding Tables

Tables contain important information. Tables often organize numbers and help you understand important information from a reading passage.

Read the following tables. Then answer the questions.

PROPORTION OF STUDENTS WHO HAD FREQUENT ('OFTEN' OR 'VERY OFTEN') CONTACT WITH SOCIAL SUPPORT NETWORK				
Person Contacted	**Freshman Year**		**Senior Year**	
	In-Person Contact	**Electronic Contact**	**In-Person Contact**	**Electronic Contact**
Mother	62%	86%	65%	86%
Father	54%	71%	57%	73%
Guardian	55%	71%	53%	67%
Siblings	50%	62%	52%	67%
High School Friends Attending the Same College	54%	53%	40%	43%
High School Friends Attending a Different College	39%	71%	32%	54%

Source: https://www.insidehighered.com/news/2007/11/05/nsse

1. What is the most common way that students keep in touch with their contacts?
   a. Through face-to-face contact
   b. Through phone, e-mail, texting, and social media

2. Which person are students more likely to contact than any other person?
   a. Their father
   b. Their mother
   c. Their brother or sister
   d. A high school friend

3. Who did students contact less and less frequently from their freshman year through their senior year in college?
   a. Their father
   b. Their mother
   c. Their brother or sister
   d. A high school friend attending the same college
   e. A high school friend attending a different college

4. Who did students contact more frequently from their freshman year to their senior year in college?

a. Their family members

b. Their friends

PROPORTION OF STUDENTS WHO FREQUENTLY FOLLOWED THE ADVICE OF FAMILY MEMBERS AND FRIENDS		
Person	Freshman Year	Senior Year
Mother	77%	73%
Father	71%	69%
Guardian	71%	70%
Siblings	45%	44%
High School Friends Attending the Same College	35%	27%
High School Friends Attending a Different College	39%	27%

Source: https://www.insidehighered.com/news/2007/11/05/nsse

1. Whose advice did students follow the most frequently?

_____

2. Whose advice did students follow the least frequently?

_____

3. What do you observe about the proportion of students who follow the advice of parents and guardians, and the proportion of students who follow the advice of their peers?

_____

Information Recall

Reread the passage and review the information in the tables. Then answer the questions.

1. What change do you observe about the students' contact with social support from their freshman year through their senior year in college?

_____

_____

2. What change do you observe in students following advice from their freshman year in college to their senior year in college?

_____

_____

3. What do the data suggest regarding the belief that many parents continue to hover when their adult children enter the workplace?

_____

_____

Writing a Summary

A summary is a short paragraph that provides the most important information in a reading. It usually does not include details, just main ideas. When you write a summary, it is important to use your own words and not copy directly from the reading.

Write a brief summary of the passage. It should not be more than five sentences. Use your own words. The first sentence of the summary is below. Write four more sentences to complete the summary.

Although people tend to believe that helicopter parenting is both common and harmful to college-age children, research indicates that it is not as serious or as widespread as they think.

_____

_____

_____

_____

_____

Another Perspective

Parental support during childhood is key to mental and physical health through adulthood

lead author Benjamin A. Shaw, *American Psychological Association*

People with abundant parental support during childhood are likely to have relatively good health throughout adulthood, whereas people with inadequate parental support while growing up are likely to have poorer health as adults, suggests a new study involving a nationally representative sample of nearly 3,000 adults.

5   Research has long shown that children who receive abundant support from their parents report fewer psychological and physical problems during childhood than children who receive less parental support. Benjamin A. Shaw, Ph.D., Assistant Professor at the School of Public Health, University at Albany and colleagues from the University of Michigan investigated for the first time whether the health effects of

10   parental support received during childhood persist throughout adulthood into old age.

The researchers analyzed responses from 2,905 adults, ages 25–74, who participated in the survey. The participants were asked about the availability of emotional support from their mothers and fathers during the years they were growing up, such as "how much could you confide in her or him about things that

15   were bothering you?" and "how much love and affection did she or he give you?" Depressive symptoms, chronic health conditions and self-esteem were also assessed through survey questions.

Results of the study indicate that adults' mental and physical health is influenced not only by current psychosocial conditions, but also by earlier life psychosocial

20   conditions dating back to childhood, including parental support. The researchers found a lack of parental support during childhood is associated with increased levels of depressive symptoms and chronic health conditions in adulthood, and this association persists with increasing age throughout adulthood into early old age.

"These findings are important because they not only reveal a strong association

25   between early parental support and adult health status, but also provide some preliminary insight into factors that link early social conditions with adult health and well-being," says Dr. Shaw. "In this study, we found that the association between early parental support and adult health may be largely due to the long-term impact of parent-child relationships on important psychosocial resources.

30   Specifically, early parental support appears to shape people's sense of personal control, self-esteem and family relationships, which in turn affect adult depressive symptoms and physical health."

If additional research supports these findings, the authors say the implications may be far-reaching for predicting who is at elevated risk for ill health in late life, and for improving the physical and mental health of older adults.

35

Questions for Another Perspective

1. What is the effect of a great deal of parental support in childhood on mental and physical health throughout adulthood?

_____

_____

2. How can a lack of parental support in childhood affect a person in adulthood?

_____

_____

3. How did the researchers investigate whether the health effects of parental support received during childhood persist into old age?

_____

_____

4. Why are the results of this study important?

_____

_____

Topics for Discussion and Writing

1. Were your parents overly involved in your life when you were growing up? If so, give examples. If not, did you feel less supported because of this? Discuss this with your classmates.

2. Work with a partner. What parts of a young adult's life—for example, personal, social, academic, professional—should parents be involved in? Are there some aspects that parents should never be involved in? Talk about this with your partner.

3. Refer to the chart on page 18. Whose advice do you frequently ask for when you need to make a decision? Do you usually ask the same people for the same kinds of advice? Why or why not?

4. Write in your journal. Do you agree that parental support in childhood is important to a person's mental and physical health in adulthood? Why or why not?

Critical Thinking

1. According to the article on pages 5–7, "Good parenting is less about pushing one's offspring to be independent at a certain age than being responsive to what a particular child needs." (lines 50–52) At what age do you think children are ready to be independent? Is this true for all children? Explain your answer.

2. Do you think parents in American culture are more involved or less involved than parents in your culture? Give examples.

3. In Another Perspective, research shows that children who receive abundant support from their parents report fewer psychological and physical problems during childhood than children who receive less parental support. What are some specific types of support that parents might give their children to ensure their mental and physical well-being in adulthood?

4. What is Alfie Kohn's purpose in presenting and discussing research on helicopter parenting? What conclusion does he come to regarding the conventional wisdom on HP?

Crossword Puzzle

Review the words in the box below. Then read the clues on the next page. Write the words in the correct spaces in the puzzle.

alarming	denunciations	impressive	involved	pervasive
caveat	diminishes	incidents	latter	plausible
claim	disparaging	indignation	nuisances	scorn
contrast	engagement	indulgence	peers	torment
counterparts	hover	intervening	perceive	

Crossword Puzzle Clues

ACROSS CLUES

7. Many students show high levels of academic _____ due to parental involvement.

9. It's natural to _____ over very young children to keep them safe

10. Parents who take an interest in a college-age child's well-being are not really being _____.

11. Given a choice between an expensive private college and an affordable public college, I would choose the _____ and save my money.

12. Many people feel a sense of _____ when others are treated better than they are.

14. _____ means giving someone whatever they want and spoiling the person.

15. A college student's classmates are his/her _____.

17. Bob has a(n) _____ opinion of parents who are overly involved in their adult children's lives.

20. I'd like to compare American college students with their _____ in other cultures.

21. Helicopter parents are often looked upon with _____. They are seen very negatively.

23. Scientists look for _____, or reasonable, explanations when analyzing their results.

24. Eventually, a student's fear of an unfamiliar campus often _____, or even disappears.

DOWN CLUES

1. Some reports wrongly _____ that parents interfere with their adult children's jobs.

2. The NSSE findings of the importance of helicopter parents were very _____.

3. Parents may incorrectly _____ the normal stress of their college-age child as depression.

4. Helicopter parenting is much less _____ than most people believe.

5. _____ of helicopter parenting are much less common than people believe.

6. It appears that the _____ of helicopter parents are not supported by research on the subject.

8. There is a big _____ between beliefs about HP and what research actually reveals.

13. Sometimes _____ with a young adult child who is struggling emotionally may be necessary.

16. It is _____ for parents to see their college-age child become depressed and anxious.

18. Some young-adult children want their parents to be _____ in their life decisions.

19. Research shows that parents do not _____, or bother, college administrators.

22. When you interpret research results, a strong _____ is to be careful about confusing an association with a direct cause/effect.

CHAPTER 2

Retirement Home Meets Day Care at Providence Mount St. Vincent

Prereading

1. How might the elderly benefit from spending time with young children?

2. How might young children benefit from spending time with the elderly?

3. Read the title of this article and look at the photo.
   a. Who are these people?
   b. Where do you think they are?
   c. What are they doing?

Reading

🎧 **Read the passage carefully. Then complete the exercises that follow.**
CD 1
TR 4

Retirement Home Meets Day Care
at Providence Mount St. Vincent

by Sami Edge, *Seattle Times*

The little boy in a bright-green shirt tightly clenches a sandwich bag and asks, "Can you open this for me?" He thrusts the bag at the elderly man seated to his right. "Sure I can, buddy," says 92-year-old David Carriere as his weathered hands reach for the bag and slowly tear at the opening. Satisfied, the little boy starts stuffing sandwiches
5   into the bag. "I haven't worked with him in a while," Carriere says. "He's smart."

On a recent Friday at Providence Mount St. Vincent retirement home in West Seattle, Washington, a group of senior citizens and youngsters are packing sack lunches that will be delivered to the homeless. It's one of many projects that bring the elderly and the young together through the Intergenerational Learning Center, a
10   day care inside the retirement home. Five days a week, children ages six weeks to five years interact with Mount St. Vincent's residents, whose average age is 92. Activities range from musical hour to story time to art classes.

Charlene Boyd, the administrator of Providence Mount St. Vincent, or "the Mount," says the Intergenerational Learning Center (ILC) was developed 23 years ago as a
15   way to further the center's mission of developing community and making the last years of life "meaningful, life-affirming and engaging." "We wanted this to be a place where people come to live, not come to die," Boyd said. "It's not rocket science," she added. "It's about normalcy."

In 1991, Boyd was part of the team that decided to open a day care at the Mount,
20   an idea that she and others thought would add to the "community" that the Mount strives to cultivate "to make from the beginning of life to the end of life the best years of life," Boyd says, "linking that full circle." Not only does interacting with children revitalize many of the residents and allow them access to a more "normal" and varied sphere, it also helps acquaint young families and children with the realities—positive
25   and negative—of aging. "It's normal for someone to use a wheelchair or a walker, and that's just part of life," Boyd said. "It's not out of sight, out of mind. It's right here. These kids see that every day, and they're not afraid."

Donna Butts, executive director of Generations United, a national group that advocates for intergenerational involvement, says the idea of intergenerational learning facilities has been around for about 25 years and shows enormous benefits. Older adults involved in the programs tend to be more optimistic, have larger social networks and better memories, and take better care of themselves, Butts says. For young people, extra attention from an older adult helps improve social skills and reduces fear of aging.

She says there are somewhere between 100 and 500 intergenerational learning facilities in the United States, and the trend is on the rise as baby boomers[1] look for stimulating and engaging care facilities for their aging parents. People are starting to wake up and smell the demographics," Butts said. "We have this older demographic and we can look at it as a problem or as an asset … people of all ages have something to give."

The ILC has proved to be a popular program. Currently, the day care is capped at 125 students and has a waiting list of two and a half years. ILC Director Marie Hoover, a former hospice provider, sees the intergenerational visits as an extension of the variety of experience that the school has to offer. Anecdotally, she says she hears often from parents who are amazed at their children's ability to interact with the elderly and disabled outside of the classroom.

"These children are pretty young, so there's not necessarily a lot of cognitive awareness," Hoover said. "But clearly, it's there." Eileen Hirami, a 13-year instructor at the day care, describes that impact in terms of the children's "emotional awareness." "From the time you're a baby to the time you die, you're an individual who wants to be recognized and respected," Hirami said. She says the children start to understand this through their daily interactions with multiple age groups—from the residents in the facility, adult volunteers in the Mount's gift shop and thrift store, teachers, and teenagers who volunteer to run the convenience store. "We have the whole spectrum of life here and it's the joy and the challenge to always be together," she says. "Sometimes it's joyful, sometimes it's stressful—how do we grow together?"

Boyd's son, Ryan Smith, was one of the first children enrolled in the day care. Now 23, he credits the program with instilling his "need to help people." Smith recently graduated from Washington State University and is studying to become a firefighter. "Looking back now, I think it's had a big impact on my life," Smith said. "It made me more aware of my surroundings and of elderly people."

Eileen McCloskey, an activities director for some of the residents, says it's unlike any other long-term-care environment she's ever worked in. "You heard all this life," McCloskey remembers of her first ILC event. "There was a joyous, raucous noise coming down the hallway that you just don't associate with long-term care." She says the residents' "eyes light up" when they interact with the children. "You just step

---

[1]**Baby boomers** refers to the 76.4 million babies born in the United States from 1946 to 1964.

back and let this magic happen," McCloskey said. "It's textbook—that's exactly why we have this program, and it's happening right here."

Victor Warkentin has two children, ages 5 and 2, enrolled in the program. He thinks the ILC philosophy, which stresses problem solving, has had an enormous impact on the way they see the world—from being able to problem solve to being more comfortable explaining their feelings and taking new chances. Warkentin sees the intergenerational aspect as an "added bonus" that just "makes the program that much better." Recently, Warkentin and his family moved from West Seattle to Issaquah. But he continues to make the trek to West Seattle. "It's worth it to me," he said. "I haven't found anything that comes close."

Statement Evaluation

Read the passage again. Then read the following statements. Indicate whether each statement is True (T), False (F), or Not Mentioned (NM). If a statement is false, rewrite it so that it is true. Then go back to the passage and find the information that supports your answers.

1. ___T___ The elderly and the children prepare lunch bags for homeless people.

_____

2. ___T___ The ILC's goal is to provide meaningful experiences for the elderly and for children.

_____

3. ___F___ Charlene Boyd believes that the period at the end of life is a person's worst years.

_____

4. ___NM___ The children play music for the elderly at the retirement home.

_____

5. ___F___ The retirement home and the day care center are in different places.

_____

6. ___F___ Most elderly in the United States live in retirement homes.

_____

7. ___T___ Children interact with the staff as well as the elderly at the retirement home.

_____

8. ___F___ The children's experiences at the retirement home have no influence on their lives as they grow up.

_____

Reading Analysis

Read each question carefully. Circle the letter or number of the correct answer, or write your answer in the space provided.

1. Read lines 8–11.

    a. **Project** means

        1. a snack or beverage.

        2. an idea or suggestion.

        3. a task or assignment.

    b. What is the **project**?

        1. Packing lunch for homeless people

        2. Having children interact with the elderly

        3. Sharing music hour and story time

    c. **Intergenerational** means

        1. young people.

        2. old people.

        3. people of all ages.

    d. The **residents** are the people who

        1. live there.

        2. volunteer there.

        3. work there.

2. Read lines 13–18.

    a. **Mission** means

        1. idea.

        2. goal.

        3. location.

    b. **Developing community** means

        1. establishing friendly relationships among people.

        2. creating a new city or town.

        3. building new housing for groups of people.

    c. **Engaging** means

        1. bearable.

        2. busy.

        3. agreeable.

d. **"It's not rocket science"** means it's
   1. hard to understand or do.
   2. easy to understand or do. *(circled)*
   3. impossible to understand or do.

e. **Normalcy** means
   1. unusualness.
   2. happiness.
   3. routine. *(circled)*

3. Read lines 19–27.
   a. **Strive** means
      1. attempt. *(circled)*
      2. hope.
      3. need.

   b. **Cultivate** means
      1. understand.
      2. support. *(circled)*
      3. find.

   c. What is the community that the Mount strives to cultivate?

      Hope communication with people of all ages

   d. **Revitalize** means
      1. give new energy to someone. *(circled)*
      2. help someone.
      3. take care of someone.

   e. **Acquaint** means
      1. protect.
      2. familiarize. *(circled)*
      3. teach.

   f. **Out of sight, out of mind** means
      1. people don't think about something unless they actually see it. *(circled)*
      2. some things are difficult to understand unless they are explained.
      3. some things are meaningless to people unless they know about it.

   g. **"These kids see that every day."** What does **that** refer to?

      Is something they get to normal.

4. Read lines 28–32.

    a. **Advocates** means

        (1.) supports.

        2. directs.

        3. discusses.

    b. In this paragraph, **social networks** refers to

        1. Instagram and Facebook.

        2. computers and tablets.

        (3.) friends and acquaintances.

5. Read lines 35–40.

    a. **Trend** means

        (1.) movement or direction.

        2. learning or teaching.

        3. helping or understanding.

    b. What **trend is on the rise**?

        engagind old people

    c. Who are **baby boomers**?

        1946-1964 people born

    d. Where did you find this information?

        Page 28

    e. This information is called a(n)

        1. preface.

        (2.) footnote.

        3. index.

    f. **Demographic** means

        1. a large part of the older population.

        (2.) a specific group of people in a population.

        3. a change in the number of people.

    g. An **asset** is

        1. a difficulty.

        2. a solution.

        (3.) a benefit.

6. Read lines 41–42. **Capped at** means

    a. filled with.

    (b.) limited to.

    c. designed for.

7. Read lines 44–46.

    a. **Anecdotally** means

        1. based on written records.

        2. based on research results.

        3. based on reports from others.

    b. **Amazed** means

        1. disturbed.

        2. astonished.

        3. satisfied.

8. Read lines 47–50.

    a. **Cognitive** means

        1. intellectual.

        2. emotional.

        3. instructional.

    b. **Impact** means

        1. training.

        2. influence.

        3. recognition.

9. Read lines 57–58.

    a. **Credits** means

        1. attributes.

        2. describes.

        3. pays.

    b. **Instilling** means

        1. teaching.

        2. inspiring.

        3. supporting.

10. Read lines 65–66. She says the residents' **"eyes light up"** when they interact with the children. This means that the residents
    a. recognize the children.
    b. turn on a light.
    c. become very happy.

11. Read lines 69–72. **Stresses** means
    a. emphasizes.
    b. pressures.
    c. explains.

12. Read lines 74–76.
    a. **Trek** means
        1. a short distance.
        2. a fast trip.
        3. a long journey.
    b. **"I haven't found anything that comes close"** means Warkentin hasn't found anything that
        1. is similar.
        2. is acceptable.
        3. is nearby.

13. What is the main idea of the passage?
    a. Intergenerational learning facilities are becoming more common in the United States.
    b. Intergenerational learning facilities are beneficial to the elderly and young alike.
    c. Intergenerational learning centers are very helpful to the communities that they are located in.

Vocabulary Skills

PART 1

> **Recognizing Word Forms**
>
> In English, there are several ways that verbs change to nouns. Some verbs become nouns by adding the suffix -ment, for example, engage (v.), engagement (n.).

Complete each sentence with the correct word form on the left. Use the correct form of the verb in either the affirmative or the negative. The nouns may be singular or plural.

amaze *(v.)*

amazement *(n.)*

1. Parents often look on in _amazement_ when the children continue to interact with the elderly outside of the classroom. The children often _amaze_ the older people with their curiosity.

develop *(v.)*

development *(n.)*

2. The mission of the Mount is the _development_ of community among people of all ages. The Mount _develops_ its facility as a center specifically for retired people.

improve *(v.)*

improvement *(n.)*

3. The older people's lives _improve_ as a result of spending time with children. The _improvement_ include having better memories and larger social networks.

involve *(v.)*

involvement *(n.)*

4. Generations United advocates for intergenerational _involvement_, an idea that has been around for about 25 years. Since the group _involves_ the elderly in these programs, the seniors have tended to be more optimistic, and take better care of themselves, too.

retire *(v.)*

retirement *(n.)*

5. After his _retirement_, David Carriere went to live at the Mount St. Vincent home. The Mount is unusual because most people _retire_ to facilities that have day care centers, too. They go to places that only have senior citizens.

PART 2

Synonyms

Synonyms are words with similar meanings. For example, *reduce* and *lessen* are synonyms.

Read each sentence. Write the synonym of the word in parentheses in the space provided. Use each word only once.

acquaint	~~meaningful~~	~~raucous~~	stresses
~~amazes~~	~~mission~~	~~satisfied~~	~~surroundings~~
~~impact~~	~~project~~		

1. The message in this biography of a struggling woman who succeeded in life is very _Meaningful_ (*relevant*) to many people.

2. This department's curriculum _stresses_ (*emphasizes*) the study of mathematics and science.

3. It was raining very hard last night, so we were _satisfied_ (*content*) to stay home and watch a movie.

4. The speed that children learn to speak always _amazes_ (*astonishes*) me.

5. My neighbors held a very _raucous_ (*loud*) party last night. I couldn't sleep.

6. My work at the hospital has had a major _impact_ (*influence*) on my view of life.

7. The teachers are helping their new students become comfortable in their new _surroundings_ (*neighborhood*).

8. We are going to start an exciting _project_ (*program*) to provide healthy breakfasts to children in need.

9. I need to _Acquaint_ (*familiarize*) you with the rules of this new game.

10. The institute's _mission_ (*purpose*) is to prepare qualified medical technicians.

Vocabulary in Context

acquainted *(adj.)*	instilled *(v.)*	residents *(n.)*	strives *(v.)*
capped *(v.)*	mission *(n.)*	revitalizes *(v.)*	trek *(n.)*
demographic *(n.)*	project *(n.)*		

Read the following sentences. Complete each sentence with the correct word from the box. Use each word only once.

1. Evan was unable to take the chemistry course because the professor __*Capped*__ the class at 25 students.

2. Most manufacturers market their products to a specific __*Demacrathic*__ to increase sales.

3. Henry's family __*Instilled*__ in him the importance of helping people who are in need.

4. When I am tired in the afternoon, a short 20-minute nap often __*Revitalizes*__ me.

5. My sister wasn't __*Acquainted*__ with jazz until she met her husband, who loves jazz.

6. The __*President*__ of that building voted to allow pets in the apartments.

7. The __*Mission*__ of that college is to help people of all ages further their education.

8. When Sue's family moved to a new city, she had to change schools. It was impossible for her to make the __*trek*__ to her old school from her new home.

9. My classmates and I are working on a new __*Project*__ together. We must make a presentation about public transportation in this city.

10. If my brother __*Strive*__ to complete his education, he will be able to get a better job than the one he has now.

Reading Skill

Organizing Information in a Chart

It is important to be able to create charts. Charts can help you organize and understand information that you read.

Read the passage again. Then complete the following chart.

The Intergenerational Learning Center (ILC)	The ILC is a day care inside the Mount St. Vincent Retirement Home.
The ILC's Mission	
The Project	Five days a week, children ages six weeks to five years interact with Mount St. Vincent's residents, whose average age is 92.
Activities and Experiences at the Intergenerational Learning Center	
Benefits to the Elderly	
Benefits to Children	

Information Recall

Review the information in the chart. Then answer the questions.

1. What is unusual about the Providence Mount St. Vincent retirement home?

_____

_____

2. What is the goal or aim of the ILC?

_____

_____

3. How does the ILC project benefit the elderly residents of the retirement home?

_____

_____

4. How does the ILC project benefit the children in the day care center?

_____

_____

Writing a Summary

A summary is a short paragraph that provides the most important information in a reading. It usually does not include details, just main ideas. When you write a summary, it is important to use your own words and not copy directly from the reading.

Write a brief summary of the passage. It should not be more than five sentences. Use your own words. The first sentence of the summary is below. Write four more sentences to complete the summary.

The Providence Mount St. Vincent retirement home has added a day care center so children and the

elderly can interact.

_____

_____

_____

_____

Another Perspective

College students are living rent-free in a Cleveland retirement home

by Heather Hansman, *Smithsonian.com*

When Laura Berick doesn't feel like walking her dog, Charlie, she asks Tiffany Tieu, who lives in her building, to take him out. The two women live in Judson Manor, a retirement home in Cleveland, Ohio. Only Tieu is a 25-year-old college student. While unique, the living arrangement has its perks for both generations. Studies have shown
5 that there are huge health benefits to the elderly—from fighting dementia to regulating blood pressure—that come from social contact with younger people. Meanwhile, college students are struggling with increasing college debts and housing costs.

Tieu, who is a second-year master's student at the Cleveland Institute of Music, is one of five students living at Judson Manor as part of an artist-in-residence program.
10 The students, who all qualify for some financial assistance, live rent-free with the 120 elderly residents of the revamped 1920s hotel. In exchange for a room, they perform solo recitals every few months as well as weekend and impromptu concerts.

The program started in 2010 with two students when a Judson board member heard about a housing shortage at the school, and it continues to expand. Next year,
15 in addition to Cleveland Institute of Music students, the retirement home is bringing in students from the Cleveland Institute of Art. Soon, students enrolled at Case Western Reserve University will be occupying some of the rooms.

The students participate in concrete ways—leading art therapy classes to help residents with dementia, for instance—but they also just hang out, which can be even
20 more valuable. Many of the residents, like Tieu and Berick, have developed close relationships. "In my everyday life I wouldn't be in touch with this group of elderly people," Tieu says. "Musically, it's really rewarding, and it lets me connect with people I otherwise would never connect with."

There's research that shows just how rewarding those connections can be,
25 especially for the older folks. A group of studies from the National Institute on Aging shows that social isolation, especially in older adults, can lead to a host of mental and physical disorders. On the other hand, the NIA reports, "Positive indicators of social well-being may be associated with lower levels of interleukin-6 in otherwise healthy people. Interleukin-6 is an inflammatory factor implicated in age-related disorders
30 such as Alzheimer's disease, osteoporosis, rheumatoid arthritis, cardiovascular disease, and some forms of cancer."

Rob Lucarelli, Judson's director of communications, says that the staff doesn't have any concrete measurement for the social and physical benefits of having younger people in the building drawing the elderly out of their rooms, but it has had a noticeably positive effect on the residents. It's tangible, and it comes from even low levels of contact, Berick says. "The people here light up when the young people walk through the lobby," she says. "It's really quite lovely." The program has also spurred interest in the home. Berick says part of what drew her to Judson in the first place is that it's close to the Cleveland Institute of Music campus, and that she could take advantage of the cultural and academic events there. She's not alone. There's a growing trend of retirement communities forging ties with nearby universities so residents can audit courses, attend performances, serve as museum docents, and use campus hospitals, libraries and fitness facilities.

Three similar programs in the Netherlands and one in Lyon, France, suggest that this model for intergenerational living could be the beginning of a new trend. The arrangements vary, but they all hinge on some kind of social interaction. At the Humanitas home in Deventer, Netherlands, younger residents are required to spend 30 hours a month helping out their neighbors.

Of her relationship with Tieu, Berick says, "We cook and sit around and talk about our problems and things that concern us. She's given me the world of a 25-year-old granddaughter, which I am scarce on."

Questions for Another Perspective

1. What is unusual about the Judson Manor retirement home?

_____

_____

2. Why don't the students pay rent?

_____

_____

3. What are the advantages of this arrangement for the residents of the retirement home?

_____

_____

4. What are the advantages of this arrangement for the college students?

_____

_____

Topics for Discussion and Writing

1. What might be some additional advantages or benefits to the elderly and the children who interact at the ILC?

2. At the ILC, children interact with people whose average age is 92. They become attached to these elderly residents, who may not live much longer. Could such an experience have adverse effects on some children? What do you think?

3. According to the article, the ILC is very popular. In fact, there is a two-and-a-half-year waiting list for children to enroll at the ILC. Why do you think there is a waiting list? What does this imply about the children's parents?

4. Write in your journal. Imagine you are one of the elderly residents of the Mount St. Vincent retirement home. Describe your experiences and feelings when you interact with the children in the day care center.

Critical Thinking

1. Charlene Boyd, administrator of the retirement home, states, "We wanted this to be a place where people come to live, not come to die." What do you think she means by this statement?

2. Charlene Boyd's son credits the ILC program with inspiring his need to help people. In what other ways do you think the ILC program may have inspired children's lives?

3. The majority of retirement communities in the United States are restricted to people 55 years old and older. What might be the advantages of these types of communities over intergenerational communities?

4. The first and second readings describe how both children and college-age students interact with residents in retirement homes. What benefits might there be to both that weren't mentioned in the readings?

5. Sami Edge, the author of the main reading, has only discussed the advantages of the retirement home/day care center. Why hasn't she discussed any possible disadvantages?

Crossword Puzzle

Review the words in the box below. Then read the clues on the next page. Write the words in the correct spaces in the puzzle.

acquaint	capped	engaging	networks	revitalize
advocate	community	instilling	normalcy	stress
amazed	credit	intergenerational	project	strives
anecdotally	cultivate	mission	residents	trend
asset	demographic			

Crossword Puzzle Clues

ACROSS CLUES

2. Parents are _____ at the social skills children develop by interacting with the elderly.

4. Developing social _____ is one of the benefits the elderly experience through the ILC.

5. The older _____ is changing as people live into their 90s and even 100s.

8. Packing lunches for the homeless is important in _____ in children the desire to help others.

11. Enrollment at this day care center is _____ at 125 children because the facilities are limited.

13. Interacting with children helps _____ the elderly who are bored with their routine lives.

14. We need to _____ strong relationships among the generations.

18. Combining retirement homes with day care centers is a(n) _____ people hope will continue.

19. The children at ILC benefit from programs that _____ problem solving and taking chances.

20. Packing lunches is one _____ that the ILC provides for the elderly and the children.

21. Developing a sense of _____ is especially important to people living in retirement homes.

DOWN CLUES

1. The ILC staff _____, or attempts, to build relationships between the young and the old.

2. Intergenerational relationships are a(n) _____, or benefit, to people of all ages.

3. The _____ nature of the ILC involves the elderly, small children, and teenagers, as well.

6. The retirement home _____ may be even older than 92 because 92 is only the average age.

7. The ILC helps _____ children with the realities of aging, such as needing a wheelchair.

9. Many organizations _____ for programs that enable young and old to interact.

10. Providing opportunities for the elderly to interact with children gives them a sense of _____.

12. _____, I often hear stories from children who love visiting the elderly and talking to them.

15. Because young children are so active, the elderly find them very _____ and fun to be with.

16. Making the last years of life meaningful is a very important _____, or goal.

17. Many adults _____ the ILC program with helping their elderly parents live better lives.

CHAPTER 3 Tablet Computers in School: Educational or Recreational?

Prereading

1. Look at the two photos. Where are the children in each photo? What are they doing?

2. Do you think the children are doing the same things in both photos? Why or why not?

3. Read the title of the chapter. What do you think the title means?

4. Should elementary school students use computers in their classes? Work in a small group. Make a list of reasons for and against computer use in elementary school. Use the chart below to organize your ideas.

Should elementary school students use computers in their classrooms?	
Yes	No
Reasons:	Reasons:

5. At what age do you think children should start learning to use a computer? Discuss this question with your classmates.

Reading

🎧 **Read the passage carefully. Then complete the exercises that follow.**

Tablet Computers in School:
Educational or Recreational?

by Matthew Godfrey, *Telegraph*

As parents of three young children and regular users of the M25[1], my wife and I know how effective tablet devices are at preventing family meltdowns in traffic jams. A spell on the iPad is normally enough to stave off sibling scrapes in the car, as well as cries of "Are we there yet?" We are always grateful for a little "iPeace" when we
5 face another delay around junctions nine and ten. But as we hand the gadget over, we have mixed feelings. There is mild guilt: shouldn't we be engaging our children in stimulating conversation or playing an inventive game to stretch their imagination? And there is apprehension, too: at some stage, the contraption will need to be wrenched back from them. The addictiveness of some games and software is such
10 that this can be like stealing a banana from a starving monkey.

The Upside of the Digital Age

I have had an iPad for a year and confess that in-car entertainment for the kids has been its principal function so far. This purpose could hardly be further removed from the one advocated by more and more schools around the country: namely, that rather than being a tool for simply pacifying children, iPads and other handheld
15 devices can—and should—be used in classrooms to unlock pupils' potential, release creativity, sustain interest and provide intellectual challenge. One of the UK's principal champions of digital learning has been Sir Anthony Seldon, Master of Wellington College in Berkshire. In 2012, he replaced the school's traditional library with one that combines "ultramodern facilities with an old-fashioned reverence for
20 learning;" interactive screens and iPads are used more than printed material for reading, research and learning. "Digitalization allows learning to be personalized and far more vivid, active and challenging for young people," says Seldon. "Shakespeare[2] would certainly have used a screen if he'd had the chance. In the hands of talented teachers, technology can be profoundly transformative."

---

[1] The **M25** is a road that encircles London.
[2] **William Shakespeare** (1564–1616) lived in England. He wrote poetry and plays, and is generally regarded as the greatest writer in the English language.

Around 500 schools across Britain have now provided pupils with iPads. Worldwide, over 10 million devices have been purchased by educational institutions—an astonishing fact given that the first iPad was only launched in April 2010. Printed textbooks are rapidly being replaced by ebooks, which harness the interactive capabilities of handheld devices and take pupils beyond the static page with a simple swipe and tap of the finger. More than 25,000 such electronic texts, covering a wealth of subjects, are now available. "The rush to adopt this new technology has led to confused launches in some schools," says Simon Armitage, a senior teacher at the Stephen Perse Foundation School in Cambridge, where iPads were introduced to all pupils two years ago. "Teachers need time to feel confident in the basic technology and its purpose in the learning process. They need to realize that an iPad offers much more than simply a connection to the Internet and a word processor."

A Trial Run with iPads in School

That is why my colleagues and I were all given an iPad and trained to use it one year before we issued them to pupils. We have had to reexamine the style, content and outcomes of our lessons, too. The school where I teach—Caterham School, in Surrey—will be issuing iPads to pupils from the start of next term. I have been struck by the positive response within the staff room to the training we have received over the past year. "I'm a bit nervous about using iPads in class for the first time," says a colleague from the math department. "But the interactive technology should make learning more memorable and engaging." One teacher of modern languages enthused: "My pupils will be able to use audio and video recorders very easily, and this will enhance the way they learn. I am sure that it will make their homework tasks more valuable and fun." "The iPads should encourage collaborative learning, which has to be good," says a teacher of politics. "The ease of communication means that classes can share ideas and resources easily. They will even be able to participate in live edebates for homework."

The Downside of Tablet Devices in School

However, there are reservations, too. Pupils will forget to bring their devices to school. They will lose them. They will break them. They will try to share inappropriate material. They will pick the wrong one up at the end of a class. Batteries will run out in the middle of lessons. "Educational" apps will be exposed as mere gimmicks. The technology will be another potential source of distraction. And however many filters, passwords and restrictions are imposed centrally, just how secure will the system be?

A central concern is that the gadgets have the potential to diminish the role of the teacher in the classroom setting. In Thailand, the government has issued every schoolchild with an iPad with the stated aim of reducing the number of teachers.

Some teacher training now uses the term "learning enabler" rather than "teacher," suggesting that the teacher's knowledge is no longer central to pupils' learning. And like many schools, Caterham promotes academic excellence, an active involvement in all aspects of school life, and a love of the outdoors—goals which, arguably, sit uncomfortably alongside the notion of more time in front of a digital screen.

Concluding Thoughts on Technology in Schools

"There are many unknowns," says John McKeown, an educational psychologist based in Brighton. "But this is no reason to abandon technology. The ballpoint pen replaced the fountain pen. The electronic whiteboard replaced the blackboard. Modern textbooks and the Internet are vast improvements over their predecessors. This latest development is no big deal for children; using electronic devices is second nature to them and, increasingly, they expect to have access to them at school. In a few years' time, most pupils will use digital technology in examinations. It is a natural and necessary next step for teachers to embrace the technology."

As a teacher of English, I will have this opportunity next week, when I will meet my new class of Year 7 pupils—each one of them armed with a shiny new tablet. I will put my experiences on the M25 behind me, and I look forward to reporting back on how we get on in my lessons.

Statement Evaluation

Read the passage again. Then read the following statements. Indicate whether each statement is True (T), False (F), or an Inference (I). If a statement is false, rewrite it so that it is true. Then go back to the passage and find the information that supports your answers.

1. ___T___ On car trips, the author and his wife give their children electronic devices so they stay calm and don't fight with each other.

   _____

2. ___F___ The author and his wife think that giving their children tablets to play with is a very good idea.

   _____

3. ___I___ The author's children use his iPad more often than he does.

   _____

4. ___T___ Sir Anthony Seldon modernized Wellington College's traditional library with new technology.

   _____

5. ___F___ Wellington College's library does not have any printed material anymore.

   _____

6. ___T___ More and more teachers around the world are using iPads with their students.

   _____

7. ___T___ The teachers at the author's school feel very positive about using iPads with their students.

   _____

8. ___IM___ Collaborative learning enhances students' experiences in school.

   _____

9. ___I___ The author has many concerns about the use of iPads in schools.

   _____

10. ___F___ New technology will be difficult for school children to learn to use.

   _____

Reading Analysis

Read each question carefully. Circle the letter or number of the correct answer, or write your answer in the space provided.

1. Read lines 1–10.

  a. A **tablet device** is

    1. a small laptop computer that can be used to make phone calls.

    (2.) a small general-purpose computer contained in a touchscreen panel.

    3. a desktop computer that can be used for business.

  b. A **meltdown** means

    (1.) an emotional upset.

    2. a car accident.

    3. a terrible argument.

  c. What is **iPeace**?

    1. A small computer that children can use to play games

    (2.) A humorous reference to quieting children with an iPad

    3. A type of device used in a car on long trips

  d. Which word in these lines is a synonym for **device**?

    ~~tool~~ contraption

  e. **Mixed feelings** means

    (1.) you have two opposite feelings at the same time.

    2. several people have the same feelings at the same time.

    3. adults have one feeling and children have another.

  f. **Stretch** means

    1. improve.

    (2.) expand.

    3. help.

  g. **Apprehension** means

    (1.) anxiety.

    2. confusion.

    3. excitement.

  h. In lines 9–10, the author means that, when he takes the iPad from his children,

    1. they will want something to eat.

    (2.) they will become very upset.

    3. they will act like monkeys.

2. Read lines 11–16.

a. **Principal** means
1. useful.
2. primary. *(circled)*
3. educational.

b. Which word in these lines is a synonym for **function**?

Purpose

c. **Pacifying** means
1. calming. *(circled)*
2. encouraging.
3. teaching.

d. Which of the following are **handheld devices**? Check (✓) all that apply.
_____ 1. laptop PC
__✓__ 2. notebook PC
__✓__ 3. ebook reader
__✓__ 4. personal digital assistant
_____ 5. television
__✓__ 6. cell phone
_____ 7. printer

3. Read lines 16-24.

a. **Digital learning** refers to
1. learning that takes place on the Internet.
2. learning that uses only handheld devices.
3. learning that utilizes technology. *(circled)*

b. **Vivid** means
1. difficult.
2. realistic. *(circled)*
3. serious.

c. Who was **Shakespeare**?

A Writer

d. Where did you find this information?

Footnote

e. This type of information is called a(n)
1. preface.
2. footnote. *(circled)*
3. index.

4. Read lines 26–34.

    a. **Astonishing** means

        1. expensive.

        2. huge.

        3. surprising.

    b. In these sentences, what is a synonym for **ebooks**?

        electronic text

    c. **Harness** means

        1. explain.

        (2.) utilize.

        (3.) demonstrate.

    d. **Launches** means

        1. opinions.

        2. purchases.

        (3.) startups.

5. Read lines 39–45.

    a. **Outcomes** means

        1. contents.

        2. results.

        3. plans.

    b. **Struck** means

        1. impressed.

        2. injured.

        3. confused.

    c. **Engaging** means

        1. challenging.

        2. appealing.

        3. educational.

6. Read lines 46–51.

    a. **Enhance** means

        1. complicate.

        2. simplify.

        3. improve.

    b. **Edebates** refers to

        1. in-class debates.

        2. online debates.

        3. written debates.

7. Read lines 52–56.

   a. **Reservations** means

      1. arrangements.

      2. advantages.

      3. doubts.

   b. **Inappropriate** means

      1. unsuitable.

      2. incomprehensible.

      3. implausible.

   c. Why is **"educational"** in quotation marks?

      1. Because the educational apps are not really educational

      2. Because the educational apps are very educational

      3. Because educational apps is a new term

   d. **Mere** means

      1. more.

      2. only.

      3. cheap.

   e. **Gimmick** means

      1. a trick or device used to sell something.

      2. something that works well.

      3. an electronic device for schools.

8. Read lines 59–60.

   a. **Potential** means

      1. importance.

      2. reason.

      3. capacity.

   b. **Diminish** means

      1. reduce.

      2. disrespect.

      3. eliminate.

9. Read lines 63–66.
   a. **Promotes** means
      1. discusses.
      2. encourages.
      3. considers.
   b. **Goals** means
      1. aims.
      2. concerns.
      3. emotions.
   c. This sentence means that
      1. Caterham's goals are in conflict with the idea of a love of the outdoors.
      2. Caterham's goals are consistent with the idea of a love of the outdoors.

10. Read lines 70–74.
   a. **Predecessor** means
      1. something that came before something else.
      2. less complicated objects or devices.
      3. much improved objects or devices.
   b. **Using electronic devices is second nature to them** means
      1. children are born knowing how to use electronic devices.
      2. using electronic devices is easy and natural for children.
      3. using electronic devices is important for children.
   c. **Embrace** means
      1. learn.
      2. enjoy.
      3. adopt.

11. What is the main idea of the passage?
   a. Many schools are adding technology in their classrooms, but some teachers have doubts about how useful it will be.
   b. Many schools are providing technology to their teachers and students, but there are some drawbacks as well as advantages.
   c. Many schools are replacing their current resources with modern technology, and this will result in fewer teachers in schools.

Vocabulary Skills

PART 1

Recognizing Word Forms

In English, there are several ways that adjectives change to nouns. Some adjectives become nouns by adding the suffix -ness, for example, useful (adj.), usefulness (n.).

Complete each sentence with the correct word form on the left. All the nouns are singular.

effective (adj.)

effectiveness (n.)

1. Researchers question the _effectiveness_ of using tablets such as iPads in the classroom. Many wonder if they are _effective_ tools for education.

vivid (adj.)

vividness (n.)

2. Sir Anthony Seldon believes that digitalization allows learning to be personalized and _vivid_ for young people. Students are often more engaged due to the _vividness_ of the material.

inventive (adj.)

inventiveness (n.)

3. The author of the article wonders if he should be playing an _inventive_ game with his children to stretch their imagination instead of encouraging them to play on their tablets. He believes that encouraging _inventiveness_ may be more valuable to his children.

nervous (adj.)

nervousness (n.)

4. Some of the author's colleagues experienced a bit of _nervous_ when using tablets for the first time. Many were _nervousness_ because they were not used to using digital devices in the classroom.

addictive (adj.)

addictiveness (n.)

5. The author of the article was worried about the _addictiveness_ of some of the games that his children played on their tablets. He felt that some of the software programs were actually _addictive_ and he should limit their use.

PART 2

Content-Specific Vocabulary

Content-specific vocabulary is very useful in understanding a particular topic, such as computer technology. For example, it is important to understand the meaning of such words as *website* and *application*.

First, match each word or phrase with the correct meaning. Then complete each sentence with the correct word or phrase. Use each word or phrase only once.

_I_   1. app (application)   a. any electronic equipment that is small enough to hold

_C_   2. digital learning   b. an electronic version of a printed book

_F_   3. digitalization   c. instruction that uses technology to enhance learning

_B_   4. ebook   d. a large interactive display connected to a computer that users control using a pen, finger, or other device

_D_   5. electronic whiteboard   e. a panel on an electronic device that responds to a user's actions

_H_   6. filter   f. the process of converting information into an electronic format

_A_   7. handheld device   g. a program that creates, edits, stores, and prints documents

_K_   8. interactive screen   h. a program that allows only certain types of information to pass through it

_M_   9. the Internet   i. programs that run on computers

_J_   10. password   j. a series of characters that allows access to a computer or an account

_I_   11. software   k. a small computer contained in a touchscreen panel

_E_   12. tablet   l. a software program that has a specific function for the user

_G_   13. word processor   m. the worldwide system that connects computers

1. The _digitalization_ of books will take many years. There are millions of books to be converted to electronic files.

2. Almost any new type of _handheld device_ is more powerful than a 15-year-old computer!

3. I need to buy some new _software_. My old programs won't work on my new computer.

4. I use a(n) _ebook_ to read when I travel, but at home I prefer to read a hard copy of a book.

5. Sonya dropped her ___tablet___ and broke it. Now she has to use her desktop computer until she gets a new one.

6. Lydia bought a new ___app___ for her cell phone that gives her local bus routes and schedules.

7. I'm tired of using a mouse. I'm going to buy a computer with a(n) ___interactive screen___ and throw my mouse away.

8. The professors at our university have begun using a(n) ___electronic whiteboard___ in their lecture classes. It's so much easier than handwriting.

9. The ___internet___ is always available. You can go online at any time.

10. My new ___word processor___ can easily create a table of contents and an index in addition to other documents.

11. You need to install a(n) ___filter___ on your child's computer so you can block websites you don't want her to access.

12. Most children today engage in ___digital learning___ in school. However, most of their parents have to learn to use digital technology on their own.

13. You need to secure your cell phone with a(n) ___password___ and never give it to anyone.

Vocabulary in Context

Read the following sentences. Complete each sentence with the correct word from the box. Use each word only once.

apprehension (n.)	~~harness~~ (v.)	~~predecessor~~ (n.)	~~reservations~~ (n.)
~~embrace~~ (v.)	inappropriate (adj.)	~~promote~~ (v.)	~~vivid~~ (adj.)
~~gimmick~~ (n.)	~~outcome~~ (n.)		

1. My little sister's nightmares were so ___vivid___ that she often awoke screaming in fear.

2. Some new cars are so small that I have ___reservations___ about their safety.

3. When their beloved boss retired, it was hard for the employees to ___embrace___ his successor.

4. Doctors ___promote___ having a healthy lifestyle in order to prevent illness.

5. Many shows on cable TV are ___Innapropiate___ for young children. Parents must monitor them carefully.

6. The students in that class are very satisfied with their new professor, who seems to be more knowledgeable than her ___predecessor___

7. Many homes in this city have solar panels on their roofs, which ___harness___ the power of the sun to generate electricity.

8. I can't wait to finish this novel. I'm excited to find out the ___outcome___ of the story.

9. When Lorna entered her college class for the first time, she was filled with both excitement and ___Apprehension___ about beginning her studies at the large university.

10. The new product that claimed to help people lose weight in just a few days was a(n) ___gimmick___. It's impossible to become thinner so quickly!

Reading Skill

Using Headings to Create an Outline

Readings often have headings. Headings introduce new ideas or topics. They also introduce details. Using headings to make an outline can help you understand and remember the most important information from the reading.

Read the passage again. Then use the sentences below to complete the outline that follows.

 Batteries will run out in the middle of lessons.

• Unlock pupils' potential.

 They will try to share inappropriate material.

A teacher of modern languages says that pupils will be able to use audio and video recorders very easily, which will make their homework tasks more valuable and fun.

Sustain interest.

In a few years' time, most pupils will use digital technology in examinations. It is a natural and necessary next step for teachers to embrace the technology.

The ballpoint pen replaced the fountain pen. The electronic whiteboard replaced the blackboard. Modern textbooks and the Internet are vast improvements over their predecessors.

 In Thailand, the government has issued an iPad to every schoolchild with the stated aim of reducing the number of teachers.

II B. A colleague in the math department feels that the interactive technology should make learning more memorable and engaging.

IV 1. Pupils will forget to bring their devices to school.

I 1. The author and his wife use handheld devices to keep their children calm on car trips.

III A. At Caterham School, teachers were given iPads and trained to use them for a year before issuing them to pupils.

II D. Digitalization allows learning to be personalized and far more vivid, active, and challenging for young people.

II 2. Release creativity.

IV 4. Even with filters, passwords, and restrictions, the system may not be secure.

Tablet Computers in School: Educational or Recreational?

I. Introduction

A. The author and his wife use handheld devices to keep---

B. They worry that they should really be talking to or playing with their children instead.

II. The Upside of the Digital Age

A. Schools around the world advocate the use of handheld devices for several purposes:

1. Unlock pupils Potential

2. Realese Creativity

3. Sustain Interest

4. provide intellectual challenge

B. Sir Anthony Seldon replaced Wellington College's traditional library with one that combines ultramodern facilities with an old-fashioned reverence for learning.

C. Interactive screens, iPads, and slates are used more than printed material for reading, research, and learning.

D. Digitalization allows learning to be

E. Around 500 schools across Britain have now provided pupils with iPads.

III. A Trial Run with iPads in School

A. At Caterham School, teachers were given I pads and trained to use them for a year before issuing them to pupils.

B. The staff have responded positively:

1. _A colleague in the math department_

2. _A teacher of modern languages says_

3. A teacher of politics says that iPads should encourage collaborative learning, and classes can share ideas and resources easily and participate in live e-debates for homework.

IV. The Downside of Tablet Devices in School

A. There are several downsides to using tablet devices in school.

1. _Pupils will forget to bring their d to school_

2. They will lose them or break them.

3. _Batteries will run out in middle of less-_

4. They will pick the wrong one up at the end of a class.

5. _They will try to share innapropiate mat._

6. "Educational" apps will be exposed as mere gimmicks.

7. The technology will be another potential source of distraction.

8. _Even with filters, pass and rest the sys may not be secure_

B. A central concern is that electronic devices have the potential to diminish the role of the teacher in the classroom.

1. _In Thailand the government_

2. Caterham promotes academic excellence, active involvement in all aspects of school life, and a love of the outdoors—goals that are not consistent with students spending more time in front of a digital screen.

V. Concluding Thoughts on Technology in Schools

A. _The Ballpoint pen replaced the_

B. This latest development is no big deal for children: using electronic devices is second nature to them and, increasingly, they expect to have access to them at school.

C. _In a few years time, most_

Information Recall

Review the information in the outline. Then answer the questions.

1. What are the author's concerns about his children's use of tablets?

   _____

   _____

2. How is digital learning more advantageous for students than traditional learning?

   _____

   _____

3. Did most of the teachers in the trial run feel that the iPads would be beneficial in the classroom? Why or why not?

   _____

4. How could the use of electronic devices diminish the role of teachers in the classroom?

   _____

Writing a Summary

When writing a summary, it is important to include only main ideas. Use your own words; do not copy from the reading.

Write a brief summary of the passage. It should not be more than five sentences. Use your own words. The first sentence of the summary is below. Write four more sentences to complete the summary.

> The author uses electronic devices to keep his children calm on car trips, but he realizes they have important educational uses, too.
>
> _____
>
> _____
>
> _____
>
> _____

Another Perspective

Read the article and answer the questions that follow.

CD 1
TR 7

Classroom Aid: Learning Scientific Concepts with iPads

by Brian Handwerk, *National Geographic News*

Just how big is the universe, how small is an atom, and how long have we humans lived on Earth compared with dinosaurs? Such answers are better learned with an iPad, according to a new study that shows just how tablets help students understand enormous scale and other difficult concepts.

5   Students saw learning gains after as little as 20 minutes of study on the iPad, the research found, and if supported with guidance from an instructor, their improvement may have been even more pronounced, the scientists suggest. "The bottom line is that these iPads and similar tools actually do make a difference," said physicist Matthew Schneps, a founding member of the Science Education Department at the Harvard-
10   Smithsonian Center for Astrophysics in Massachusetts. "What we were testing is, does the iPad actually allow you to simulate things that students couldn't otherwise experience?" Schneps pointed to a realistic demonstration of the solar system on the tablet as one such example of something that can be difficult to explain in a classroom. Tapping the unique powers of these devices unleashed neurocognitive learning
15   capabilities in the brain that aren't often used during traditional instruction, he added.

Let Your Fingers Do the (Star) Walking

In the study, high school students in Bedford, Massachusetts, used the Solar Walk simulation from Vito Technology to explore a 3-D, pinch-to-zoom display in two different ways, Schneps explained. First, the display was set so that the solar system appeared in the unrealistic "orrery display" scale that's commonly depicted
20   in textbooks, and an Earth orbit shrunk to just five times the size of the planet's own diameter. The second experience used a true-to-scale mode, showing how tiny planets actually are, compared with the size of their orbits, appearing as mere dots on the screen to show viewers just how vast the solar system really is. Users showed improved learning when using both modes, the authors reported, but the true-scale experience
25   was particularly effective in promoting learning and clearing up scale misconceptions.

Next Steps

The research suggests that tablets could aid the study of many scientific concepts that are difficult to grasp, such as distance, time, and other large-scale subjects, said

Schneps. "These occur in the study of geologic time, the size and age of the universe, the timeframe of biological mutation and evolution, the mass, size, and speed of subatomic, atomic, and molecular particles, and so on," the study noted.

While this type of learning remains in its infancy, tapping the technology may one day become critical career training for young and future generations. "They're not going to be doing things in their jobs the same way that previous generations did," Schneps said. "So if kids can learn in schools today using the same tools that they will use in their careers later on, that's a good thing."

Questions for Another Perspective

1. What is one of the most important uses of an iPad?

   _____

   _____

2. What were the results of Matthew Schneps' research with students using iPads?

   _____

   _____

3. Briefly, what two experiences did the students have in the study?

   _____

   _____

4. What do the results of the research suggest?

   _____

   _____

5. Why might this type of learning be so important?

   _____

   _____

Topics for Discussion and Writing

1. Matthew Godfrey uses his tablet device to keep his children quiet on long car trips, but he feels guilty that he and his wife aren't interacting with them. Do you think that the parents should be communicating with the children instead? Give reasons for your answer.

2. Why does Sir Anthony Seldon feel that Shakespeare would have used a screen (that is, an electronic device)?

3. Imagine that you have a child who is asking to use a tablet device. Will you give it to your child? Why or why not? If yes, for how long and for what purpose?

4. Write in your journal. What do you think is the ideal age for a child to be introduced to computers? Why?

Critical Thinking

1. In the first reading, Matthew Godfrey states that his school, Caterham, promotes academic excellence, an active involvement in all aspects of school life, and a love of the outdoors. He says that these goals are not consistent with students spending more time using electronic devices. How might these two very different goals be met?

2. A central concern is that electronic devices will reduce the role and the number of teachers in the classroom. Do you think this concern is justified? Explain the reasons for your answer.

3. In the first reading, Simon Armitage, a senior teacher at the Stephen Perse Foundation School, says this about handheld devices: "The rush to adapt this new technology has led to confused launches in some schools." (page 50, lines 31–32) Why do you think there is a rush for schools to adapt to new technology?

4. In the second reading, Matthew Schneps describes his recent research. He states that the students experienced learning gains, and with the assistance of teachers, might have learned even more. Do you think that future research will support the need for teachers in the classroom, even with the use of computers?

5. The tone of a reading is the author's emotion or feeling towards the subject. What is the tone of Matthew Godfrey's article regarding the usefulness of electronic devices for school-age children?

Crossword Puzzle

Review the words in the box below. Then read the clues on the next page. Write the words in the correct spaces in the puzzle.

apps	embrace	gadget	launches	principal
astonishing	engaging	gimmicks	outcomes	promote
diminish	enhance	goals	password	reservations
ebooks	filter	inappropriate	potential	vivid
effectiveness	function			

Crossword Puzzle Clues

ACROSS CLUES

3. The ___Principal___ purpose of computers in school should be education, not recreation.

5. Few people will argue that computers ___enhance___ learning when used properly.

7. Research shows that computers can ___Promote___ learning with teacher guidance.

10. What is the primary ___Function___ of a handheld device in classrooms?

12. Some electronic devices are not useful. They are just expensive ___Gimmicks___.

13. Some educators have ___reservations___ about issuing breakable handheld devices to students.

15. There have been many ___Launches___ of new electronic devices over the past several years.

16. My cell phone is a useful ___gadget___ for calls, texts, and Internet access.

19. Most teachers ___embrace___ technology and will use it if given training and opportunities.

21. Handheld devices have the ___Potential___ to improve learning if they are used wisely.

22. Sustaining interest and releasing creativity are two ___outcomes___ of classroom computer use.

DOWN CLUES

1. Children find learning on computers very ___engaging___. They can sit with them for hours.

2. Computers display ___vivid___ images that facilitate understanding of difficult subjects.

4. Children should not be exposed to ___Inappropriate___ material on websites.

6. It is truly ___astonishing___ how quickly technology has advanced in the past 20 years.

8. Teachers' role in the classroom may ___Diminish___ one day, but they can never be replaced.

9. I need to change my ___password___ on my iPad. My current one will expire soon.

11. Research has demonstrated the ___effectiveness___ of careful computer use in schools.

14. Tim's parents put a(n) ___Filter___ on his iPad to screen unsuitable websites.

17. One of the ___goals___ of digitalization is to provide greater access to information worldwide.

18. I like reading ___Ebooks___ when I travel, but at home I prefer to read hard copies.

20. How many ___Apps___ do you have on your iPad for banking, shopping, or travel?

Influences on Our Lives: Nature vs. Nurture

1. Are some children born with special gifts, or can they learn them as they grow?

2. Do hospitals sometimes make mistakes with their patients? What kinds of mistakes do they make?

3. How long does the average person live? Are there things we can do to live longer lives?

Prereading

1. On your own, write a definition of a *gifted child*.

2. As a class, review your descriptions and combine them into a single definition.

3. Below is the definition of a child prodigy. Compare this with your class's definition of a gifted child. How is your class definition similar? How is it different?

   Child prodigy: someone under the age of 13 who is capable of excelling in at least one area of skill at a level that is considered to be an adult level in that field. There are child prodigies in all different skill areas including music, math, chess, the arts, and even humanities. As long as the child shows demonstrable adult-level skill in one of these areas prior to that age 13 mark, he or she is considered a prodigy in that area.

4. Look at the title of the reading. What do **you** think makes a child a prodigy? Work with a partner and write your answers in the chart below.

   _____

   _____

   _____

   _____

Reading

🎧 **Read the passages carefully. Then complete the exercises that follow.**

What makes a child prodigy?

What is the secret to having a gifted child? How important is the environment in which these children are raised? Can parents actually help their children become gifted, or is genius inborn? The following passages explore the many questions surrounding child prodigies.

Are gifted children born or made?
by Susan Logue, *Voice of America News*

Some say given enough time, money, and instruction, any child can develop a
5   special expertise. Others, however, insist that gifted children are born, not made.

A Rage to Master
Gaven Largent, 13, has been playing music for five years. He started with guitar
lessons at age eight, but not long after, he quit—not making music, just taking lessons.
"I wasn't learning anything," he says. "I was just playing those notes on the paper; it
was boring."
10   "Gaven became frustrated that it was sheet music and he was only playing the
notes on the music," his mother Melissa says. "He wanted to fill it in and make it
more." She says they knew when he was nine or ten that music would be his focus.
"It became an obsession for him to figure out the sounds that he heard on a CD or the
radio or live music."
15   That obsession is one of the trademarks of a gifted child, or prodigy, according to
developmental psychologist Ellen Winner, who teaches at Boston College. "I say they
have a rage to master. It is difficult to tear them away from the area in which they
have high ability."

Looking Back as Former Child Prodigies
Julian Lage, who is now 21, remembers playing guitar for hours as a child. "You
20   wake up and you eat and you play music and you sleep." Lage, who recently released
his first CD, *Sounding Point,* started playing guitar at five. A few years later, he was
the subject of a documentary film, *Jules at Eight.* Still, the title "child prodigy" was
something he never felt he could relate to. "Younger musicians, my contemporaries
who have been called child prodigies, they feel slighted because it does undermine
25   the work ethic, the thousands of hours you put in just to be able to produce a sound
on your instrument."

That is a sentiment echoed by Rasta Thomas, 27, who was also labeled a prodigy. He made dance history as a teenager, winning the Gold Medal in the Senior Men's Division of the prestigious Jackson International Ballet Competition in Jackson, Mississippi, at the age of 14. He now headlines his own dance company, Bad Boys of Dance. "I think if you give any seven-year-old the training I had, you will get a product that is at the top of its game," Thomas says. "I have had hours and hours and a million dollars invested into the training that I received."

Enabling Talent to Flower

But Ellen Winner, the author of *Gifted Children: Myths and Realities,* disagrees. "You can't make a gifted child out of any child." Winner says prodigies are born with natural talent, but she does believe they "need to be enabled in order to have their ability flower." Both Julian Lage, who played with vibraphonist Gary Burton at age 12, and Rasta Thomas, who studied at the Kirov Ballet Academy in Washington, say they had that support. But the success that both Lage and Thomas enjoy today as adults is due to much more. Winner says studies have shown that most music prodigies are unheard of as adults. "The gift of being a child prodigy is very different from the gift of being an adult creator," she says. "To be an adult creator means you have to do something new, which means taking a risk." Both Lage and Thomas took that creative risk early, composing and choreographing while they were still in their teens. Gaven Largent is headed in that direction as well. "I do write," he says. "I haven't written too many songs with lyrics, but that's something I'd like to work on." Right now, he adds, he is working on a gospel song.

The Role of Families

by Ellen Winner, Excerpted from *Child Prodigies and Adult Genius: A Weak Link*

The notion that giftedness is a product of intensive training reflects an overly optimistic view of the power of nurture. A more negative view of the power of nurture is reflected in another common claim—that gifted children are created by driving, overambitious parents. There is concern that the end result of such extreme pushing will be disengagement, bitterness, and depression. Parents of such children are often told to let their children have a normal childhood.

But most gifted children do not become bitter and disaffected. Moreover, it is impossible to drive an ordinary child to the kinds of high achievements seen in gifted children. In addition, gifted children typically report that their family played a positive, not negative, role in their development. We know quite a bit about the family characteristics of gifted children, at least of those in our society, today. These characteristics are positive ones, as described below, but the research does not allow us to conclude that particular family characteristics play a causal role in the development of giftedness.

The families of gifted children are child-centered, meaning that family life is often totally focused on the child's needs. But the fact that parents spend a great deal of time with their gifted child does not mean that they create the gift. It is likely that parents first notice signs of exceptionality, and then respond by devoting themselves to the development of their child's extraordinary ability. And of course we have no information on the number of child-centered families that do not produce gifted children.

Gifted children typically grow up in "enriched" family environments with a high level of intellectual and/or artistic stimulation. We cannot conclude that stimulation and enrichment lead to the development of giftedness. First, gifted children may need an unusual amount of stimulation and may demand enriched environments, a demand to which their parents respond. Thus, the child's inborn ability could be the driving force, leading the child to select an enriched environment. Parents of gifted children typically have high expectations, and also model hard work and high achievement themselves. But it is logically possible that gifted children have simply inherited their gift from their parents, who also happen to be hard-working achievers.

Parents of gifted children grant their children more than the usual amount of independence. But we do not know whether granting independence leads to high achievement, or whether it is the recognition of the child's gift that leads to the granting of independence. It is very possible that gifted children are particularly strong-willed and single-minded, and thus demand independence.

Eight-year-old blind prodigy Ying-Shan Tseng performs at the Pioneer School for the Blind in Worcester, South Africa.

Statement Evaluation

Read the passage again. Then read the following statements. Indicate whether each statement is True (T), False (F), or an Inference (I). If a statement is false, rewrite it so that it is true. Then go back to the passage and find the information that supports your answers.

1. _____ People disagree on whether gifted children are born or made.

   _____

2. _____ Gaven Largent took guitar lessons for a long time.

   _____

3. _____ Ellen Winner believes that gifted children have a "rage to master."

   _____

4. _____ Julian Lage doesn't like being called a child prodigy.

   _____

5. _____ Julian Lage worked very hard to become successful.

   _____

6. _____ Rasta Thomas believes he is a successful dancer because he was a child prodigy.

   _____

7. _____ Most music prodigies do not become very successful as adults.

   _____

8. _____ Parents of gifted children always push their children hard to succeed.

   _____

9. _____ Parents of gifted children are probably successful people.

   _____

Reading Analysis

Read each question carefully. Circle the letter or number of the correct answer, or write your answer in the space provided.

1. Read lines 2–3.

    a. **Genius** means

        1. an ability to learn something well.

        2. the ability to act like an adult.

        3. great intelligence or ability.

    b. **Inborn** means

        1. intelligent.

        2. genetic.

        3. educated.

2. In line 5, **expertise** means

    a. gift.

    b. skill.

    c. lesson.

3. Read lines 6–11.

    a. **Not long after** means

        1. a short time later.

        2. a long time later.

        3. as soon as.

    b. Why did Gaven quit taking lessons?

_____

    c. **Frustrated** means

        1. sad.

        2. bored.

        3. irritated.

4. Read lines 13–16.

    a. What was Gaven's **obsession**?

        1. Taking guitar lessons

        2. Playing the guitar

        3. Figuring out the sounds he heard in music

    b. An **obsession** is

        1. a constant preoccupation with something.

        2. an ability to learn something quickly.

        3. a great love of music.

c. **Trademark** means
   1. a musical quality.
   2. a unique characteristic.
   3. a gifted child.

5. Read lines 19–22.

   a. "**You wake up and you eat and you play music and you sleep.**" This sentence means that Julian Lage
      1. never went to school.
      2. didn't sleep a lot.
      3. played music all day.

   b. A **documentary** film
      1. is based on facts.
      2. is always historical.
      3. is a serious drama.

6. Read lines 23–26.

   a. **Contemporaries** means
      1. classmates.
      2. peers.
      3. musicians.

   b. Who are Julian's **contemporaries**?

      _____

   c. **Slighted** means
      1. misunderstood.
      2. disliked.
      3. ignored.

7. Read lines 27–30.

   a. **Sentiment** means
      1. feeling.
      2. complaint.
      3. wish.

   b. **Prestigious** means
      1. world-renowned.
      2. highly respected.
      3. child-centered.

8. Read lines 31–32. "**I think if you give any seven-year-old the training I had, you will get a product that is at the top of its game.**" This sentence means that with proper training, any child can

   a. always be a winner.

   b. become a good player.

   c. reach the highest level of performance.

9. Read lines 34–35. Winner believes child prodigies **"need to be enabled in order to have their ability flower."** In this sentence, **flower** means
   a. improve.
   b. grow.
   c. show.

10. Read lines 40–42. **Winner says studies have shown that most music prodigies are unheard of as adults.** This sentence means that most music prodigies
    a. don't become famous when they're adults.
    b. don't want to hear music as adults.
    c. are unhappy as adults.

11. Read lines 48–52.
    a. In these sentences, what word is the opposite of **optimistic**?

    _____

    b. **Disengagement** means
       1. anger.
       2. disappointment.
       3. withdrawal.

12. Read lines 54–56.
    a. **Disaffected** means
       1. dissatisfied and separate.
       2. excited and eager.
       3. depressed and angry.
    b. **To drive** means to
       1. take someone by car.
       2. push someone to do something.
       3. allow someone to become something.
    c. The second sentence means that
       1. an ordinary child cannot be made to become gifted.
       2. an ordinary child can be made to become gifted.

13. Read lines 62–63. What is a **child-centered** family?

    _____

14. In line 65, **exceptionality** means
    a. uniqueness.
    b. intelligence.
    c. talent.

15. Read lines 69–70.

   a. **Enriched** means

      1. wealthy.

      2. enhanced.

      3. child-centered.

   b. **Stimulation** means

      1. encouragement.

      2. education.

      3. instruction.

16. What is the main idea of these articles?

   a. It is impossible for a child to become a prodigy unless he is born with special abilities.

   b. Children can become prodigies if they receive the right amount of family support.

   c. People disagree about whether nature or nurture is responsible for giftedness in a child.

Vocabulary Skills

PART 1

Recognizing Word Forms

In English, there are several ways that nouns change to adjectives. Some nouns become adjectives by adding the suffix -al, for example, *music (n.)*, *musical (adj.)*. There may be spelling changes as well.

Complete each sentence with the correct word form on the left. The nouns may be singular or plural.

intellect *(n.)*

intellectual *(adj.)*

1. Child prodigies are born with high levels of _____ and are enriched by both artistic and _____ stimulation in their family life.

parent *(n.)*

parental *(adj.)*

2. Overly ambitious _____ can sometimes drive their children to bitterness and depression. However, all children, regardless of their giftedness, need _____ support in order to flourish.

environment *(n.)*

environmental *(adj.)*

3. In addition to genetics, there are _____ factors that can affect a child's intelligence. According to Ellen Winner, a child-centered home _____ can help a child develop her extraordinary ability.

cause *(n.)*

causal *(adj.)*

4. In her article, Ellen Winner questions whether positive family characteristics play a _____ role in the development of child prodigies. She also questions if intensive training is one of the many _____ of giftedness.

nature *(n.)*

natural *(adj.)*

5. Winner says prodigies are born with _____ talent, but need to be enabled in order to have their ability grow. In other words, talent may be a result of _____ , but nurturing of the talent is needed as well.

PART 2

Phrasal Verbs

A phrasal verb is a verb plus an adverb, a preposition, or both. Phrasal verbs have a different meaning from the original verb. *Grapple with, care for, fill up, bring up, back off, get on with, look back on, get back to,* and *run out of* are common phrasal verbs.

First, match each phrasal verb with the correct meaning. Then complete each sentence with the correct phrasal verb. Use the past tense if necessary, and use each phrasal verb only once.

_____	1. figure out		a.	complete
_____	2. fill in		b.	concentrate on
_____	3. focus on		c.	give rise to
_____	4. grow up		d.	identify with
_____	5. head in		e.	invest
_____	6. lead to		f.	leave with difficulty
_____	7. put in		g.	mature
_____	8. relate to		h.	move in
_____	9. tear away from		i.	solve
_____	10. work on		j.	undertake (or take up)

1. As children _____ (*mature*), their dependence on their families decreases.

2. Julian Lage, who is now 21, can easily _____ (*identify with*) younger musicians who have been called child prodigies.

3. In order to apply for the job, you must _____ (*complete*) this application.

4. Many child prodigies are so obsessed with the area of their high ability, that it's hard for them to _____ themselves _____ (*leave with difficulty*) it.

5. I'm going to _____ (*undertake*) taking some online classes so that I can further my education.

6. It was difficult for the students to _____ (*solve*) the complicated mathematical equation.

7. Because of my sister's interest in government, she will _____ (*concentrate on*) politics and law in her university classes.

8. A good education can _____ (*give rise to*) a better position in most companies.

9. If you want to be a successful pianist, you must _____ (*invest*) a lot of time and energy to practicing every day.

10. Like Julian Lage, Gaven Largent hopes to _____ (*move in*) the direction of composing his own music.

Vocabulary in Context

contemporaries (*n.*)	frustrated (*adj.*)	sentiment (*n.*)	stimulation (*n.*)
disaffected (*adj.*)	inborn (*adj.*)	slighted (*adj.*)	trademark (*n.*)
expertise (*n.*)	obsession (*n.*)		

Read the following sentences. Complete each sentence with the correct word from the box. Use each word only once.

1. Because of my cousin's _____ in computer technology, I asked him for help when I had a problem with my laptop.

2. Many students become _____ when they study in another country and are unable to communicate easily in their new language.

3. In most birds, the ability to fly is _____.

4. It's important for young children to receive a lot of intellectual _____ from their parents to help them develop cognitively.

5. Kenzi felt _____ when all of her classmates went to lunch without her.

6. The _____ of an effective doctor is his willingness to listen carefully to each patient's concerns.

7. The _____ employee made an appointment to speak to the manager about his problems at the company.

8. The students were sad on the last day of class, and their teacher shared their

_____ .

9. Carlos has a(n) _____ with playing computer games. He plays them every day for hours after school.

10. The talented writer enjoyed discussing his work with his _____ .

Reading Skill

Organizing Information in a Chart

It is important to be able to create charts. Charts can help you organize and understand information that you read.

Read the passage again. Then complete the following chart.

ARE GIFTED CHILDREN BORN OR MADE?		
Name of prodigy:	How does this person excel?	How does this person feel about being called a child prodigy? Why?
1.		
2.		
3.		

Name of psychologist:
Does she believe gifted children are born or made? Why?
What does she say about child prodigies as adults?
What role does the family play in a gifted child's development?

Information Recall

Review the information in the chart. Then answer the questions.

1. What characteristics do all three child prodigies have in common?

   _____

   _____

2. What are some ways that gifted children often feel about being labeled child prodigies?

   _____

   _____

3. What does Ellen Winner think about making a gifted child out of an ordinary child?

   _____

   _____

4. What types of family support do child prodigies often get?

   _____

   _____

Write a brief summary of the passage. It should not be more than five sentences. Use your own words. Be sure to indent the first sentence.

Another Perspective

Read the article and answer the questions that follow.

CD 1
TR 9

How does insight help gifted children?

by Brendan L. Smith, *American Psychological Association*

Insight—that spontaneous moment of inspiration that helps solve difficult problems—may be one reason that gifted students excel in academics more than their peers, says Matthew McBee, Ph.D. "That's counter to what you're trained to do in school, which is to always keep trying, rather than taking your attention away from the problem to allow insight to happen," he says. "If you're engaging in insight, you won't get any closer to the solution until it pops into your mind."

McBee, an assistant professor of experimental psychology at East Tennessee State University, will recruit 40 students from a high school in Johnson City, Tennessee— half from a gifted student program and half from general classes. The students will be tested on association problems, a word association task that measures insight in problem solving. One problem could ask students to think of a word related to three other words, such as "bank," "book" and "pad." (The correct answer is "note" to produce "bank note," "notebook" and "notepad.")

The study participants will answer questions about their mood, frustration level and progress on solving each problem. McBee will monitor their heart rates to see if their heart rate jumps just before an "aha moment" of insight, a result found in previous studies by Norbert Jausovec, Ph.D., at the University of Maribor in Slovenia.

McBee will equip study participants with a head tracker—a cap with a video camera on top—to measure how often students look away from the computer screen to focus on something other than the test problem. Such breaks, known as incubation, allow for the possibility of insight, McBee says. He expects to find that gifted students have more incubation experiences and less frustration than students who are not gifted. The results may inform educators on better ways to reduce frustration for both gifted and non-gifted students during difficult tasks, he says.

Meanwhile, Carlton Fong, a doctoral student in educational psychology at the University of Texas at Austin, wants to help educators design better programs for gifted students. He will conduct a meta-analysis of the effectiveness of programs designed to help underachieving gifted students by boosting their self-esteem, increasing their motivation, or improving their study habits and time management skills.

"A lot of these psychosocial interventions have had powerful effects," Fong says. "Hopefully, this study will offer a push for more collaboration in this area to get the most effective results."

Questions for Another Perspective

1. How do gifted students solve problems differently from the way that students are usually taught to solve problems?

   _____

   _____

2. Why will Dr. McBee recruit students for his study from both gifted student programs and general classes?

   _____

   _____

3. What is incubation? How does it allow for the possibility of insight?

   _____

   _____

4. What will Carlton Fong study? Why?

   _____

   _____

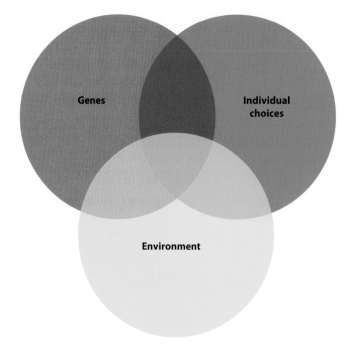

Topics for Discussion and Writing

1. In this chapter, different people give their opinions about the question of whether prodigies are born or made. Whose viewpoint do you agree with? Why? Explain your answer.

2. Some child prodigies go to universities when they are extremely young. Do you think this is a good environment for these children? Why or why not? Explain your answer, and give examples to support your opinion.

3. To what degree do you think genes, individual choices, and environment influence us as we mature? For example, do you think they affect us equally, as in the graphic above? Discuss this with your classmates. Create a new graphic that illustrates your ideas.

4. Write in your journal. Imagine you discover that your young son or daughter is a child prodigy. What will you do? How will you encourage your child? How will you protect your son or daughter's childhood?

Critical Thinking

1. Does Rasta Thomas believe he is successful because he was a child prodigy? Why or why not?

2. Is the special ability of child prodigies due to nature, nurture, or both? Explain your answer.

3. In Another Perspective, how are the goals of Carlton Fong's and Dr. McBee's studies similar? What is their attitude about education for both gifted and non-gifted students?

4. Some people say that with enough time, money, and instruction, any child can develop a special expertise. Others, however, insist that gifted children are born, not made. What is Ellen Winner's opinion about gifted children? Does she believe they are born, made, or both? Explain your reasons for your answer.

Crossword Puzzle

Review the words in the box below. Then read the clues on the next page. Write the words in the correct spaces in the puzzle.

contemporaries	enriched	frustrated	obsession	sentiment
disaffected	exceptionality	genius	optimistic	slighted
disengagement	expertise	inborn	parental	stimulation
documentary	flower	natural	prestigious	trademark
drive				

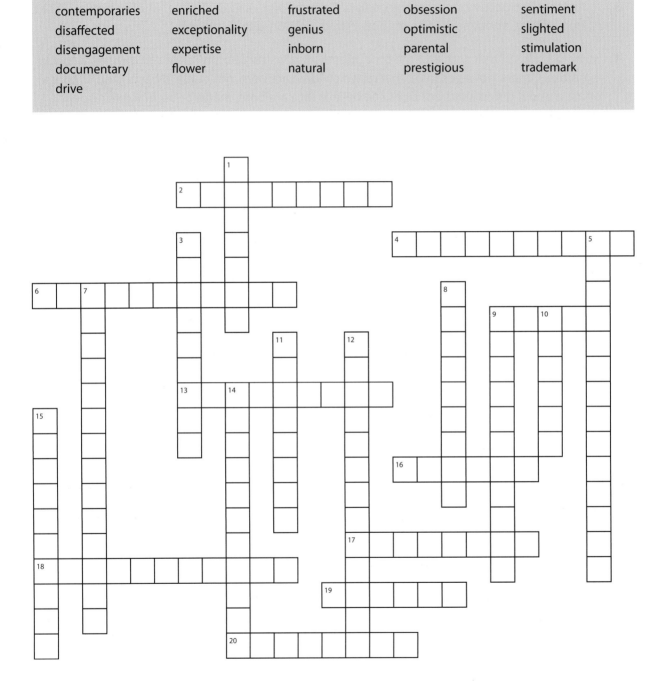

Crossword Puzzle Clues

ACROSS CLUES

2. The _____ of a true professional is the ability to learn from others without feeling hurt.

4. Child prodigies often become _____ when they have to do boring activities.

6. I am going to make a(n) _____ film about the life of a famous musician.

9. Developmental psychologists warn parents not to _____ their children too hard to succeed.

13. I have no _____ in the field of child psychology. I need to speak to an expert.

16. Given the proper environment, a child's inborn talent can _____ .

17. The children's lives were _____ by a house filled with books, art, and music.

18. All children need _____ for them to do well in school and in life.

19. Albert Einstein was a(n) _____ who developed the theory of relativity.

20. Vanessa felt _____ when the teacher paid more attention to other students.

DOWN CLUES

1. It is very _____ for gifted children to focus on their particular talent.

3. I know how you feel, but I do not share your _____ . I have a different opinion.

5. Teachers often identify _____ in children because they are with them all day.

7. Our _____ , or peers, can be very important to us as we grow up.

8. A(n) _____ is a constant preoccupation with something to the exclusion of everything else.

9. The employees became very _____ when management ignored their complaints about unsafe working conditions.

10. Giftedness is _____ , not something that can be developed.

11. _____ support is very important for all children, not only gifted children.

12. Children often experience _____ , or withdrawal, when they do not do well in school.

14. The Juilliard School is a very _____ school for music and dance.

15. Carla is _____ that she will get a full music academy scholarship because she is so talented.

Prereading

1. What types of mistakes are tragic? Why are they tragic?

2. What does being switched at birth mean?

3. Look at the photo and read the title of the article. What do you think happened to the two women in the framed photographs? How do you think this happened?

Reading

🎧 **Read the passages carefully. Then complete the exercises that follow.**

CD 1
TR 10

Tragic Mistakes: When Children Are Switched as Babies

In cities all over the world, babies in hospitals are sometimes given to the wrong mothers. These mistakes don't happen very often. However, when they do occur, these mistakes cause anguish and pain, and frequently result in legal action as parents try to reclaim their biological children.

Babies Switched at Birth Will Not Be Returned to Their Biological Families
by Sam Masters, *Independent*

5   For three years the parents of "Girl M" and "Boy Z" had little idea they were nurturing one another's children. The children—born on the same day in August 2010 at Tambo Memorial Hospital in Johannesburg, South Africa—were swapped at birth. This was only discovered 18 months ago when one of the mothers sued her boyfriend for maintenance arrears.

10   The man denied being the child's father. To settle the dispute, DNA tests were ordered and it emerged that neither the woman nor the man in question was, in fact, a biological parent of the child. What followed was a legal battle that has gripped South Africa. It reached a conclusion this week with a judge in Pretoria ruling that the two children, now five, will stay with the families who raised them and will not be

15   returned to their "true" parents.

    The couples the children now live with are the "psychological" if not the "biological" parents of Girl M and Boy Z, the court ruled. The children will now be considered to have been adopted by the parents who brought them up, said Anne Skelton, director at the University of Pretoria's Centre for Child Law, the court's

20   advisers. "Now it is as if they are the children of the parents with which they are living," she told *Reuters*. "Nobody is fighting it. Three of the parents totally agree with the decision. One father is uncertain, but he said through his lawyers that he would abide by the decision of the court."

    How the children were mixed up at the Johannesburg hospital remains in doubt.

25   Local reports suggest that a nurse at the hospital had switched the name tags of the two babies. Still, it is unclear how having a differently sexed baby could have been explained. One of the mothers had reportedly wanted her biological child back but had been persuaded to accept the court ruling, with access to the other child. One of

the fathers also expressed concern about the cultural problems of raising a son from a different clan. He was a Zulu and the other family were Pedi.

A South African legal expert, Professor Thandabantu Nhlapo, said performing certain rituals would "make things right with the ancestors". His report to the court reportedly identified three such rituals—naming the child, introducing the child to the ancestors and fortifying the child against illnesses—that could aid the situation. Deputy Judge President Aubrey Ledwaba said there had been no "winner" in the case before the court. "It is not a matter where anyone can say they've won. It is a matter which must, at the end of the day, benefit the children," he said.

Damages Awarded to Families of Girls Swapped as Babies
by Michael Leidig, *Telegraph Media Group*

A court in Poland has awarded almost £350,000 (US $584,600) in damages to the families of two girls who were mistakenly swapped by hospital staff when they were babies. The ruling in Warsaw brings to a close a seven-year battle for the families after their daughters discovered their true identities.

Kasia and Nina Ofmanska, who are identical twins, were taken to a Warsaw hospital after developing pneumonia in 1983, when they were two weeks old. While they were there, staff mistakenly switched Nina with another girl, Edyta Wierzbicka. Neither set of parents noticed and, as the "twins" grew up, doctors explained their startling differences by claiming that they had never been identical.

The separated twins grew up just a few miles from each other in Warsaw and were only reunited when an old school friend of one of the girls said she had another friend who was the spitting image of her. Kasia and Nina—now adults—came face to face and the shocking truth began to unravel. "Oh God, she was just like me. We even walk the same way," said Kasia. Nina added: "We were seeing each other for the first time, but I felt as if I knew everything about her."

Now their parents are trying to piece their family back together after the court ruling ended their struggle to force Poland's medical authorities to admit their error. Both sets of parents have received counseling. The twins were born prematurely to their mother, Elzbieta Ofmanska, in one hospital while Edyta's mother, Halina Wierzbicka, gave birth at a nearby clinic on December 15, 1983. But all three premature babies developed lung infections and were transferred separately to a third hospital, the Saskiej Kepie Clinic, at which Nina and Edyta were mixed up.

Warning bells started to sound almost immediately when Nina's real mother was told by doctors that a slight foot deformity she had been born with had miraculously cured itself. "People always ask us how on earth it was possible that we didn't notice that Nina wasn't Nina," Mrs. Ofmanska said. "But you have to understand that she

65 went into an incubator[1] as soon as she was born. As they grew up, the Ofmanska "twins" grew more and more different.

"Nina—or the girl we thought was Nina—was very shy, calm and law-abiding. But Kasia was more boisterous and more emotionally an extroverted. She never played with dolls but liked to get out of the house, to ski and sail." It was only when the
70 friend introduced the separated twins, aged 17, that the truth finally dawned. They had got the same exam grades at school and had boyfriends with the same name.

The real Nina then met her birth parents and the two families realized what had happened in the hospital. While the twins were delighted at their reunion, the parents were devastated and angry. Mrs. Ofmanska said of her rediscovered daughter: "I gave
75 birth to her, but after that I missed the whole of my daughter's childhood and can never get it back. It's hard to believe that she was here in our home, as a tiny baby, for just nine days after she came home from hospital. But after that we lost her, we weren't there for her for 17 years."

---

[1] An **incubator** is a type of medical equipment used to provide special care for sick or premature babies.

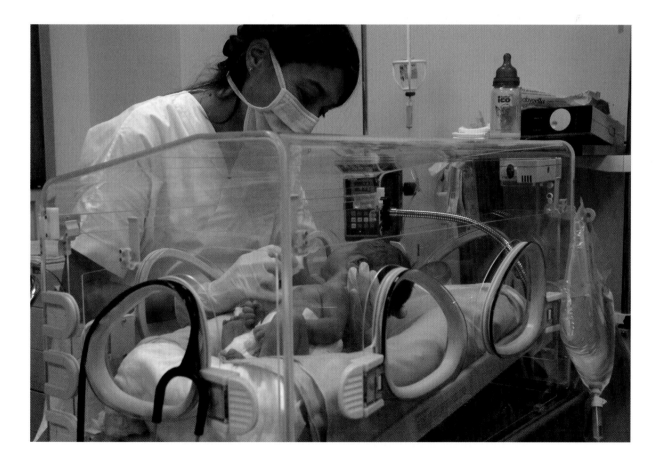

Statement Evaluation

Read the passage again. Then read the following statements. Indicate whether each statement is True (T), False (F), or Not Mentioned (NM). If the statement is false, rewrite it so that it is true. Then go back to the passage and find the information that supports your answers.

1. _____ The families of the baby boy and the baby girl in South Africa did not know they had the wrong child for almost two years.

_____

2. _____ The South African woman who sued her boyfriend was shocked to learn that she was not the child's biological mother.

_____

3. _____ The South African man who denied being the baby's father really was the baby's father.

_____

4. _____ No one is sure just how any of the babies were switched.

_____

5. _____ The parents of the switched children in South Africa performed rituals to help the situation.

_____

6. _____ The families of Kasia and Nina Ofmanska were the first to discover that they were twins and had been switched as babies.

_____

7. _____ Edyta Wierzbicka is not one of the twins switched as babies.

_____

8. _____ Edyta and one of the twins looked different from each other.

_____

9. _____ An old school friend told Kasia and Nina that they were twin sisters.

_____

10. _____ Poland's medical authorities were willing to admit their mistake.

_____

Reading Analysis

Read each question carefully. Circle the letter or number of the correct answer, or write the answer in the space provided.

1. Read lines 2–4.
   a. **Anguish** means
      1. confusion.
      2. grief.
      3. expense.
   b. **Reclaim** means
      1. recover.
      2. identify.
      3. raise.

2. Read lines 5–9.
   a. **Nurturing** means
      1. holding.
      2. exchanging.
      3. caring for.
   b. **Swapped** means
      1. switched.
      2. taken.
      3. traded.
   c. **Maintenance** refers to money that must be paid
      1. to support a child.
      2. to repair a home.
      3. to a lawyer.
   d. **Arrears** are
      1. parents.
      2. laws.
      3. debts.

3. Read lines 10–12.
   a. **Denied** means
      1. said it was impossible.
      2. refused to accept.
      3. did not want.

b. **Emerged** means
   1. became known.
   2. came as a surprise.
   3. came as a tragedy.

4. Read lines 13–15. **"True"** means
   a. legal.
   b. claimed.
   c. biological.

5. Read lines 17–20. **Considered** means
   a. regarded.
   b. taken.
   c. told.

6. Read lines 22–23. **Abide by** means
   a. agree with.
   b. go along with.
   c. be happy with.

7. Read line 24. **In doubt** means
   a. unclear.
   b. in court.
   c. a mistake.

8. Read lines 27–28.
   a. One of the biological mothers
   1. wanted her biological child back.
   2. wanted to keep her nonbiological child.
   b. This biological mother
   1. kept the child she had been given by mistake.
   2. did not keep the child she had been given by mistake.
   c. **Access** to the other child means
   1. the right to hear about the other child.
   2. the right to spend time with the other child.
   3. the right to take the other child back.

9. Read lines 28–30.
   a. A **clan** is
      1. a group of related people.
      2. a local organization.
      3. a large community.
   b. Zulus and Pedi are
      1. related clans.
      2. unrelated clans.
   c. Zulus and Pedi
      1. have similar cultures.
      2. have different cultures.

10. Read lines 31–34. **Rituals** means
    a. words.
    b. ceremonies.
    c. dances.

11. Read lines 45–46.
    a. **Startling** means
       1. usual.
       2. normal.
       3. astonishing.
    b. The two babies
       1. looked very similar.
       2. did not look similar.

12. Read lines 47–50.
    a. When someone is **the spitting image of** someone else,
       1. they look exactly the same.
       2. they dislike each other.
       3. they somewhat resemble each other.
    b. **The truth began to unravel** means
       1. the truth became more complicated.
       2. the truth slowly became clear.
       3. the truth became hidden again.

13. Read lines 55–60.

   a. **Born prematurely** means

     1. born at about the same time.

     2. born before their due date.

     3. born with health conditions.

   b. **Transferred** means

     1. relocated.

     2. hospitalized.

     3. treated.

14. Read lines 61–65.

   a. **Warning bells started to sound** means

     1. someone realized that something was wrong.

     2. alarms went off in the hospital.

     3. doctors found a problem with the baby.

   b. **Deformity** means

     1. infection.

     2. malformation.

     3. difference.

   c. **Miraculously** means

     1. amazingly.

     2. completely.

     3. suddenly.

   d. **Cured** means

     1. changed.

     2. healed.

     3. helped.

   e. What is an **incubator**?

_____

   f. Where did you find this information?

_____

   g. This type of information is called a(n)

     1. index.

     2. footnote.

     3. definition.

15. Read lines 67–70.

   a. **Boisterous** means

      1. noisy.

      2. nervous.

      3. offensive.

   b. **Extrovert** means

      1. brave.

      2. athletic.

      3. sociable.

   c. **The truth finally dawned** means the twins

      1. wanted to learn the truth.

      2. looked exactly the same.

      3. realized the true story.

16. Read lines 73–74.

   a. **While** means

      1. although.

      2. at the same time.

      3. during.

   b. **Delighted** means

      1. relieved.

      2. thrilled.

      3. interested.

   c. **Devastated** means

      1. angry.

      2. relieved.

      3. distressed.

17. What is the main idea of the passage?

   a. Hospitals sometimes mistakenly switch babies and give them back to the wrong families.

   b. When hospitals mistakenly switch babies, it sometimes leads to legal action and causes considerable distress among the parents.

   c. When hospitals erroneously switch babies, they never admit their mistakes and try to keep the children from their biological parents.

Vocabulary Skills

PART 1

Recognizing Word Forms

In English, there are several ways that verbs change to nouns. Some verbs become nouns by adding the suffix -ance or -ence, for example, differ (v.), difference (n.). There may be spelling changes as well.

Complete each sentence with the correct word form on the left. Use the correct form of the verb in either the affirmative or the negative. All the nouns are singular.

maintain *(v.)*

maintenance *(n.)*

1. When two parents divorce, it's common for one parent to pay
   _____ to the parent the child lives with. This money helps to
   _____ support of the child.

accept *(v.)*

acceptance *(n.)*

2. One of the mothers in the first article wanted her biological child back. She
   _____ the court ruling against her. However, her eventual
   _____ of the court's decision was based on her being given
   access to her birth child.

occur *(v.)*

occurrence *(n.)*

3. Instances of babies being switched at birth _____ very
   often. Fortunately, the _____ of these tragic mistakes is
   quite rare.

emerge *(v.)*

emergence *(n.)*

4. In the first article, after DNA tests were done, it _____
   that the man was not the child's biological father. In fact, neither he nor
   the woman was the natural parent. The _____ of this
   information was devastating!

transfer *(v.)*

transference *(n.)*

5. The incident in Poland happened when doctors _____
   the three premature babies to another hospital. The result of the
   _____ was that two of the babies were inadvertently switched.

PART 2

Content-Specific Vocabulary

Content-specific vocabulary is very useful in understanding a particular topic, such as law. For example, it is important to understand the meaning of such words as *judge* and *illegal*.

First, match each word or phrase with the correct meaning. Then complete each sentence with the correct word or phrase. Use each word or phrase only once.

_____ 1. abide by (*v.*)

_____ 2. arrears (*n.*)

_____ 3. award (*v.*)

_____ 4. court ruling (*n.*)

_____ 5. damages (*n.*)

_____ 6. dispute (*n.*)

_____ 7. law-abiding (*adj.*)

_____ 8. legal action (lawsuit) (*n.*)

_____ 9. settle (*v.*)

_____ 10. sue (*v.*)

a. an amount paid as compensation for loss or injury

b. bring legal action against someone

c. comply with; follow

d. decide by a court of law to give compensation to someone

e. a disagreement between parties over a legal right

f. obeying the law

g. a formal legal demand for one's rights

h. a judicial decision

i. payments past due

j. resolve a lawsuit

1. No one was surprised by the _____. The evidence made it clear that the man had deliberately set fire to the house.

2. I have never had to _____ anyone. I hope I never have to take anyone to court!

3. My father is a(n) _____ citizen. He has never broken any laws.

4. The man's former wife took him to court because he was six months in

_____ on his child support payments.

5. Once a judge has made a decision in court, all parties must _____ the decision. However, they can appeal by asking a higher court to reverse the decision.

6. The employee threatened to take _____ against her employer because she felt she had been fired unfairly.

7. That case never went before a judge. The two parties decided to _____ their disagreement out of court.

8. Sometimes courts decide that millions of dollars in _____ should be given to someone who was harmed by illegal business actions.

9. The neighbors could not resolve their _____ between themselves, so they went to court to resolve their argument.

10. The court decided to _____ the two people $100,000 as compensation for the injuries they had sustained in a car accident.

Vocabulary in Context

boisterous *(adj.)*	denied *(v.)*	reclaimed *(v.)*	startling *(adj.)*
considered *(v.)*	devastated *(v.)*	ritual *(n.)*	swapped *(v.)*
delighted *(adj.)*	doubts *(n.)*		

Read the following sentences. Complete each sentence with the correct word from the box. Use each word only once.

1. When the police mistakenly arrested the innocent man, he _____ that he had robbed a bank.

2. That city was _____ by the tornado. Many homes and businesses were completely destroyed.

3. William Shakespeare is _____ to be the greatest writer in the English language.

4. Paolo recently moved because his former neighbors threw _____ parties every weekend and played loud music until 3 a.m.

5. The loud clap of thunder was so _____ that my dog jumped up and ran under the bed!

6. Sina was _____ when she saw the delicious dinner her father had prepared for her while she was at school.

7. The meteorologist predicts a large snowstorm for tomorrow, but I have my _____ that it will happen since it's very warm and sunny today.

8. After losing the gold medal in the swimming competition last year, Adam finally _____ first place in the swimming competition last week.

9. Brian discovered that his new textbook was missing some pages, so he returned to the bookstore and _____ it for another one.

10. Before Klio goes to bed at night, she cleans the kitchen, feeds her cat, and locks the doors. She follows the same _____ every evening.

Reading Skill

Creating a Chain of Events

A chain of events shows the order in which events take place. Creating a chain of events makes any cause and effect relationships clear, and helps you understand and remember information from a reading passage.

Reread the passage. Use the sentences below to complete each chain of events.

The Case in South Africa

- A judge rules that the two children will stay with the families who raised them.
- The man denies being the child's father. A court orders DNA tests.
- "Girl M" and "Boy Z" are given to the wrong parents and taken home.
- The child's parents, and the mother's true biological child, are identified.
- The mother sues the boyfriend for maintenance arrears.

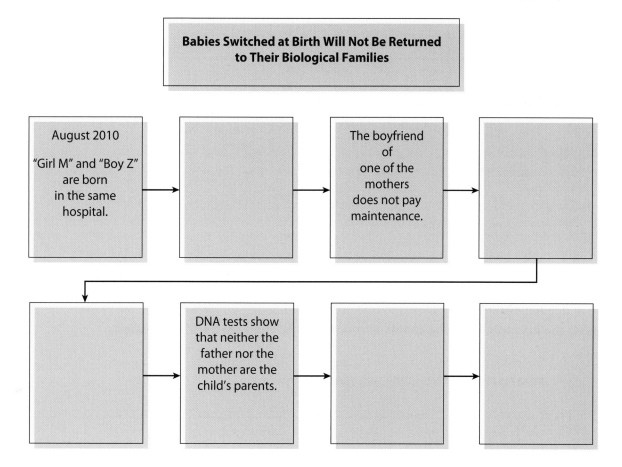

The Case in Poland

- The real Nina meets her birth parents, and the two families realize what has happened.
- All three babies develop lung infections and are transferred to a third hospital.
- A Polish court awards $584,600 in damages to the two families.
- The girls meet and realize they are twins.
- Nina and Edyta are switched and taken home to the wrong families.

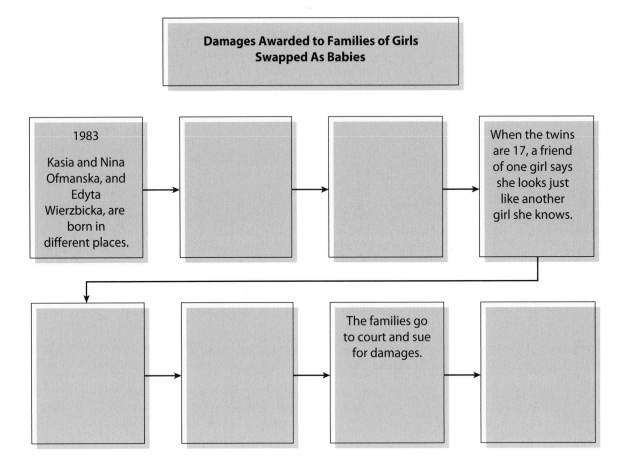

Information Recall

Review the information in the chains of events above. Then answer the questions.

1. What was similar about the two cases?

2. What was different about the two cases?

_____

_____

3. How did the switch in the first case become known?

_____

_____

4. How did the switch in the second case become known?

_____

_____

5. How was each case resolved in court?

_____

_____

Writing a Summary

When writing a summary, it is important to include only main ideas. Use your own words; do not copy from the reading.

Write a brief summary of the passage. It should not be more than five sentences. Use your own words. Be sure to indent the first sentence.

_____

_____

_____

_____

_____

_____

_____

Mercedes Casanella is reunited with her biological son

Another Perspective

🎧 **Read the article and answer the questions that follow.**
CD 1
TR 11

El Salvador Babies Switched at Birth, Back with Parents Three Months Later

by Rafael Romo and Erin McLaughlin, *CNN*

When Mercedes Casanella gave birth to her baby boy in a San Salvador hospital, she noticed he had lighter coloring like his father. But when the time came to go home, she thought the baby she was given looked different, with a darker complexion. There was a good reason for her confusion: It wasn't her child.

5 Three months later, TV news cameras captured Casanella and her husband reconnecting with their own son—a reunion that came after an investigation involving prosecutors, doctors, police, and DNA experts. At the same time Monday, the infant boy that Casanella and her husband, Richard Cushworth, had taken was reunited with his own birth parents.

10 This roller coaster of emotions started in May when Cushworth, who is British, and Casanella, who is from El Salvador, welcomed their son Jacob into the world.

The couple, who live in Dallas, said Jacob's skin coloring had resembled that of his lighter-skinned father. That's unlike the baby given to them by hospital staffers, who told them that the color change was natural and nothing to worry about. But that
15 explanation didn't satisfy Casanella and Cushworth, who took their suspicions to authorities.

Salvadoran prosecutors found out there had been four babies born at the same hospital the day Casanella gave birth. They ordered DNA tests for all of them. Dr. Josefina Morales de Monterrosa, from the Legal Medicine Institute of El Salvador, was
20 in charge of conducting the tests. She said that when the DNA sample of a baby given to another couple was compared with that of Cushworth and Casanella, there was a match. "We obtained absolute compatibility with a 99.9999 probability, which means that the paternity and maternity are practically proven," Morales said. "This is the highest index of probability of paternity in these types of cases."

25 Authorities are trying to figure out exactly how and why this happened. Police have arrested Dr. Alejandro Guidos, the gynecologist who delivered baby Jacob. Guidos claims that he's innocent of any wrongdoing. He was released on bond, but authorities have ordered him not to leave El Salvador. The mix-up also spurred Salvadoran authorities to order a review of protocols followed at public and private
30 hospitals in the country to prevent this from happening again.

The other family involved has chosen not to speak about the case publicly. Authorities are withholding their identities to respect their wishes and to protect the rights of their baby. Yet Cushworth and Casanella have spoken out. Most recently, they focused not on their months-long struggle but their happy reunion as well as
30 their gratitude for their family members and friends back home in Texas. "There are no words to express what our hearts feel to have our baby at home!" the couple said in a statement.

Questions for Another Perspective

1. Why were Mercedes Casanella and Richard Cushworth suspicious when the hospital staffers gave them their child?

_____

_____

2. Why did the prosecutors order DNA tests for the four babies?

_____

_____

3. How did this switch occur?

_____

_____

4. What are the authorities in El Salvador doing to prevent this kind of mix-up from happening again?

_____

_____

Topics for Discussion and Writing

1. One of the mothers was persuaded to keep her nonbiological child. She would, however, have access to her biological child. Do you think this was a fair solution for her? Why or why not?

2. Deputy Judge President Aubrey Ledwaba said that the case "is a matter which must, at the end of the day, benefit the children." (page 96, lines 36–37) Do you agree with this statement? Why or why not?

3. How can hospital personnel prevent errors such as the ones described in this chapter? Work with a partner. Create a list of guidelines that must be followed by hospital doctors, nurses, and other staff to avoid mistakenly switching babies. Compare your guidelines as a class. Draft a set of regulations for hospital personnel to follow.

4. Write in your journal. You are a parent and have raised your child from birth, believing that he or she was really yours. One day you discover that your child, who is now an adult, is not your biological son or daughter, but was switched at birth. How would you feel? What would you do?

Critical Thinking

1. Why was one father in Johannesburg concerned about keeping his nonbiological child? What actions might he take to resolve this problem?

2. Deputy Judge President Aubrey Ledwaba said there had been no winner in the South African case. What does he mean by this? Do you agree with him? Why or why not?

3. Think about the case of the switched children in Johannesburg. As a court adviser, would you have made the same decision or a different decision? Explain your reasons.

4. The Polish twins were delighted that they had been reunited, but all the parents were devastated. Why might the twins and the parents have such different feelings?

5. In Another Perspective, Cushworth and Casanella have spoken out about the case publicly, but the other family involved has chosen not to. Why do you think the other family made this decision?

6. Compare the tone of Sam Masters' article with the tone of Michael Leidig's article. Are they similar in tone, or are they different? Give examples to support your answer.

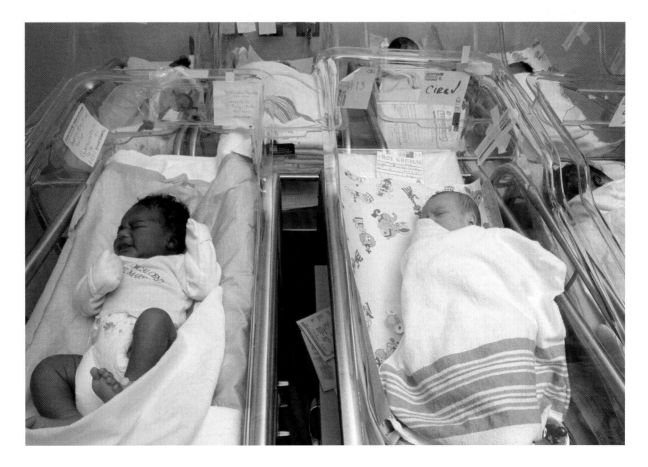

Crossword Puzzle

Review the words in the box below. Then read the clues on the next page. Write the words in the correct spaces in the puzzle.

accepted	boisterous	devastated	miraculously	settle
access	consider	dispute	nurturing	startling
anguish	damages	emerged	occurrence	transferred
arrears	delighted	extrovert	rituals	while
award	denies	maintenance		

Crossword Puzzle Clues

ACROSS CLUES

1. The people next door were so _____ during their party that their neighbors called the police.

4. I have an old car. The _____ is expensive. It costs me $1,000 a year in repairs.

7. Anna is a(n) _____. She enjoys parties, singing, dancing, and meeting new people.

9. The children were _____ by the games and activities at the birthday party.

11. Unfortunately, _____ some people eventually find their biological child, others do not.

16. Finding out you have a long-lost twin must be a(n) _____ and exciting discovery.

17. The company took back my car because I was $1,000 in _____ on my car payments.

19. _____ are important in all cultures, and every culture has ceremonies for special occasions.

20. People who adopt children _____ the children as their own and love them just as much.

21. After investigating the evidence, the identity of the true killer _____, and she was arrested.

22. When people are reasonable, they can usually resolve a(n) _____ without going to court.

DOWN CLUES

2. Fortunately, the accidental switching of babies in a hospital is a rare _____.

3. The two men decided to _____ their disagreement without going to court.

4. I thought I had lost my expensive necklace. _____, I found it three months later!

5. I cannot imagine the _____ a parent must feel to have a child switched at birth.

6. When a man _____ he is the father, a DNA test can prove whether or not he is.

8. Children need careful _____ to grow up happy and healthy.

10. The family was _____ by the loss of their house when it burned down in a fire.

12. The doctors _____ the very ill woman to a hospital that specialized in her condition.

13. The families _____ the money that the Polish court decided was due to them.

14. When courts _____ money in a court case, the loser in the lawsuit must pay the money.

15. When a court decides a case, _____ due are usually money, but could be something else.

18. In some cases, a child lives with one parent and the other is permitted _____ to the child.

Prereading

1. In groups of three or four, speculate on how long the average person lives. Discuss factors that affect a person's longevity, both positively and negatively. For example, diet is a factor. How can diet positively affect your longevity? How can it negatively affect your longevity? Use the chart below to help you organize your ideas.

Factors	Positive Effects	Negative Effects
diet		

2. After you have organized the factors, prepare a brief (two- or three-minute) report that one of you will present to the class.

3. After all the groups have presented their views, work in your group again. Revise your chart as needed and then report any changes to the class.

4. Read the title. Who do you think the article will say lives longer?

Reading

🎧 **Read the passage carefully. Then complete the exercises that follow.**

CD 1
TR 12

Who lives longer?

by Patricia Skalka, *McCall's*

How to live longer is a topic that has fascinated mankind for centuries. Today, scientists are beginning to separate the facts from the fallacies surrounding the aging process. Why is it that some people reach a ripe old age and others do not? Several factors influencing longevity are set at birth, but surprisingly, many others are
5   elements that can be changed. Here is what you should know.

Some researchers divide the elements determining who will live longer into two categories: fixed factors and changeable factors. Gender, race and heredity are fixed factors—they can't be reversed, although certain long-term social changes can influence them. For example, women live longer than men—at birth, their life
10   expectancy[1] is about seven to eight years more. However, cigarette smoking, drinking, and reckless driving could shorten this advantage.

There is increasing evidence that length of life is also influenced by a number of elements that are within your ability to control. The most obvious are physical lifestyle factors.

Health Measures

15   According to a landmark study of nearly 7,000 adults in Alameda County, California, women can add up to seven years to their lives and men 11 to 12 years by following seven simple health practices: (1) Don't smoke. (2) If you drink, do so only moderately. (3) Eat breakfast regularly. (4) Don't eat between meals. (5) Maintain normal weight. (6) Sleep about eight hours a night. (7) Exercise
20   moderately.

Cutting calories may be the single most significant lifestyle change you can make. Experiments have shown that in laboratory animals, a 40 percent calorie reduction leads to a 50 percent extension in longevity. "Eating less has a more profound and diversified effect on the aging process than does any other lifestyle change," says
25   Byung P. Yu, Ph.D., professor of physiology at the University of Texas Health Science Center at San Antonio. "It is the only factor we know of in laboratory animals that is an anti-aging factor."

---

[1]**Life expectancy** is a measure of how long persons may live based on the year of their birth.

Psychosocial Factors

A long life, however, is not just the result of being good to your body and staving off disease. All the various factors that constitute and influence daily life can be critical too. In searching for the ingredients to a long, healthy existence, scientists are studying links between longevity and the psychological and social aspects of human existence. The following can play significant roles in determining your longevity.

Social Integration

Researchers have found that people who are socially integrated—they are part of a family network, are married, participate in structured group activities—live longer. Early studies indicated that the more friends and relatives you had, the longer you lived. Newer studies focus on the types of relationships that are most beneficial. "Larger networks don't always seem to be advantageous to women," says epidemiologist Teresa Seeman, Ph.D., associate research scientist at Yale University. "Certain kinds of ties add more demands rather than generate more help."

Autonomy

A feeling of autonomy or control can come from having a say in important decisions (where you live, how you spend your money) or from being surrounded by people who inspire confidence in your ability to master certain tasks (yes, you can quit smoking, you will get well). Studies show these feelings bring a sense of well-being and satisfaction with life. "Autonomy is a key factor in successful aging," says Toni Antonucci, associate research scientist at the Institute for Social Research at the University of Michigan.

Stress and Job Satisfaction

Researchers disagree on how these factors affect longevity. There isn't enough data available to support a link between stress and longevity, says Edward L. Schneider, M.D., dean of the Andrus Gerontology Center at the University of Southern California. Animal research, however, provides exciting insights. In studies with laboratory rats, certain types of stress damage the immune system and destroy brain cells, especially those involved in memory. Other kinds of stress enhance immune function by 20 to 30 percent, supporting a theory first advanced by Hans Selye, M.D., Ph.D., a pioneer in stress research. He proposed that an exciting, active and meaningful life contributes to good health.

The relationship between job satisfaction and longevity also remains in question. According to some researchers, a satisfying job adds years to a man's life, while volunteer work increases a woman's longevity. These findings may change as more women participate in the workforce. One study found that clerical workers suffered twice as many heart attacks as homemakers. Factors associated with the coronary problems were suppressed hostility, having a nonsupportive boss, and decreased job mobility.

Environment

Where you live can make a difference in how long you live. A study by the California Department of Health Services in Berkeley found a 40 percent higher mortality rate among
65 people living in a poverty area compared to those in a nonpoverty area. "The difference was not due to age, sex, health care or lifestyle," says George A. Kaplan, Ph.D., chief of the department's Human Population Laboratory. The resulting hypothesis: A locale can have environmental characteristics, such as polluted air or water, or socioeconomic characteristics, such as a high crime rate and level of stress, that make it unhealthy.

Socioeconomic Status

70 People with higher incomes, more education and high-status occupations tend to live longer. Researchers used to think this was due to better living and job conditions, nutrition and access to health care, but these theories have not held up. Nevertheless, the differences can be dramatic. Among women 65 to 74 years old, those with less than an eighth-grade education are much more likely to die than are women who
75 have completed at least one year of college.

What Can You Do?

The message from the experts is clear. There are many ways to add years to your life. Instituting sound health practices and expanding your circle of acquaintances and activities will have a beneficial effect. The good news about aging, observes Erdman B. Palmore of the Center for the Study of Aging and Human Development at Duke
80 Medical Center in North Carolina, is many of the factors related to longevity are also related to life satisfaction.

Statement Evaluation

Read the passage again. Then read the following statements. Check whether each statement is True (T), False (F), or Not Mentioned (NM). If a statement is false, rewrite it so that it is true. Then go back to the passage and find the information that supports your answers.

1. _____ There is nothing you can do to increase longevity.

_____

2. _____ Laboratory rats that exercised lived longer than those that did not exercise.

_____

3. _____ Eating less may help you live longer.

_____

4. _____ There may be a connection between longevity and psychological factors.

_____

5. _____ Women who work outside the home have more heart attacks than working men do.

_____

6. _____ People who live in poverty areas live longer than people who live in nonpoverty areas.

_____

7. _____ People with higher socioeconomic status tend to live longer than those with lower socioeconomic status.

_____

Reading Analysis

Read each question carefully. Circle or check the letter or number of the correct answer, or write your answer in the space provided.

1. Read lines 1–5.
   a. Which word means the opposite of **facts**?

   _____

b. How do you know?

_____

c. People who **reach a ripe old age** are people who
   1. die young.
   2. are women.
   3. live a long time.
d. Which word is a synonym of **factors**?

_____

2. Read lines 6–10.
   a. **Fixed** means
      1. changeable.
      2. unchangeable.
   b. **Fixed factors** are those that
      1. we can change.
      2. we are born with.
      3. can be reversed.
   c. What follows the dashes (—)?
      1. Explanations
      2. Causes
      3. New ideas
   d. **Reversed** means
      1. influenced.
      2. changed back.
      3. eliminated.
   e. What are examples of **certain long-term social changes**?

_____

   f. How is **life expectancy** defined?

_____

3. Read lines 15–20.
   a. **Landmark** means
      1. very significant.
      2. very big.
      3. very detailed.
   b. **If you drink, do so only moderately.** In this sentence, **do so** means
      1. smoke.
      2. eat.
      3. drink.

c. **Moderately** means
  1. socially.
  2. reasonably.
  3. practically.
d. **If you drink, do so only moderately**. What does this sentence mean?
  1. Do not drink.
  2. Drink as much as you want.
  3. Drink only a little.
e. **Maintain normal weight** means
  1. stay at a reasonable weight.
  2. lose weight if you can.
  3. gain only a little weight.

4. Read lines 22–27.
a. **Extension** means
  1. decrease.
  2. change.
  3. increase.
b. **Profound** means
  1. deep.
  2. encouraging.
  3. physical.
c. "**It** is the only factor we know of in laboratory animals that is an anti-aging factor." In this sentence, what does **it** refer to?
  1. Lifestyle change
  2. Eating less
  3. Extension in longevity
d. This sentence means that in experiments with laboratory animals, cutting calories
  1. is the only proven element in helping extend longevity.
  2. is one of several proven elements in helping extend longevity.
  3. may be an important element in helping extend longevity.

5. Read lines 30–32.
a. **Ingredients** means
  1. results.
  2. aspects.
  3. components.
b. **Links** means
  1. connections.
  2. studies.
  3. concepts.
c. What does **the following** refer to?

d. **Determining** means
      1. decreasing.
      2. influencing.
      3. revealing.

6. Read lines 33–39.
   a. What word is a synonym for **ties**?

   _____

   b. **Demands** are
      1. responsibilities you feel for yourself.
      2. claims others make on you.
      3. stress you feel from inside.
   c. **Generate** means
      1. benefit.
      2. connect.
      3. produce.
   d. What does research show about social integration? Check (✓) all that apply.
      1. _____ Having friends and relatives can extend your life.
      2. _____ The types of relationships you have may be more important than the number.
      3. _____ Married people tend to live longer than single people.
      4. _____ Sometimes relationships may be more harmful than beneficial.
      5. _____ Larger networks are sometimes not beneficial to women.
      6. _____ Larger networks are always beneficial to men.

7. Read lines 40–46.
   a. **Autonomy** means
      1. having control over decisions in your life.
      2. being able to live on your own.
      3. being happy living alone without help.
   b. **Having a say** means
      1. having an opinion.
      2. having a choice.
      3. speaking loudly.
   c. **Key** means
      1. successful.
      2. single.
      3. significant.

8. Read lines 47–62.
   a. What does **these factors** refer to?

   _____

b. **Enhance** means
  1. improve.
  2. satisfy.
  3. change.
c. **The relationship between job satisfaction and longevity also remains in question.**
  This sentence means
  1. job satisfaction may only contribute to longevity if it is volunteer work.
  2. job satisfaction may only increase men's longevity.
  3. researchers are not sure how job satisfaction contributes to longevity.
d. The **coronary problems** are
  1. heart attacks that most women workers had.
  2. heart attacks that the homemakers had.
  3. heart attacks that the clerical workers had.
e. **Hostility** means
  1. sadness.
  2. anger.
  3. dissatisfaction.

9. Read lines 63–76.
  a. **Mortality rate** refers to
  1. illness rate.
  2. survival rate.
  3. death rate.
  b. In these lines, a synonym for **area** is

  _____

  c. A **hypothesis** is a
  1. theory.
  2. fact.
  3. law.
  d. Which socioeconomic factor affects the longevity of women 65 to 74 years old more than any other factor?
  1. Better living conditions
  2. Better job conditions
  3. A higher education
  4. Better access to health care

10. What is the main idea of the passage?
  a. Many factors influence our longevity, including age, gender, heredity, as well as work, education, and relationships.
  b. Many factors influence our longevity and we can take steps to change some of them so we can live longer, more satisfying lives.
  c. We can change some factors in our lives and if we do, we will live much longer.

Vocabulary Skills

PART 1

Recognizing Word Forms

In English, there are several ways that verbs change to nouns. Some verbs become nouns by adding the suffix *-ion* or *-tion*, for example, *fascinate (v.), fascination (n.)*. There may be spelling changes as well.

Complete each sentence with the correct word form on the left. Use the correct form of the verb in either the affirmative or negative. All the nouns are singular.

reduce *(v.)*

reduction *(n.)*

1. When researchers _____ the amount of food they gave the laboratory mice, they found that the mice lived longer as a result of the _____ in calories.

integrate *(v.)*

integration *(n.)*

2. Social _____ is an essential component in living longer. If we _____ ourselves into social groups such as our family or friends, we reduce our chances of living longer lives.

separate *(v.)*

separation *(n.)*

3. Further research will help us _____ fact from fiction in deciding what we can do to live better, longer lives. The _____ of reality from myth is very important.

determine *(v.)*

determination *(n.)*

4. The quality of our relationships _____ our life expectancy, not the number. The _____ of benefits is not difficult. Do the relationships satisfy us?

satisfy *(v.)*

satisfaction *(n.)*

5. Most people look for a job that _____ their need to feel important and happy. The level of job _____ may or may not lead to extended life expectancy, however.

destroy *(v.)*

destruction *(n.)*

6. In studies with rats, researchers found that some kinds of stress can lead to considerable _____ of brain cells. However, other types of stress _____ brain cells. Rather, they enhance the immune system.

PART 2

Read each sentence. Write the synonym of the word in parentheses in the space provided. Use each word only once.

advanced	fallacy	instituted	profound
autonomy	hostility	link	sound
factor	hypothesis		

1. José has developed very _____ (*strong*) health practices since he found out he has a heart condition.

2. Alma felt so much _____ (*anger*) toward her boss that she had to leave her job and find another one.

3. Thinking that all stress is harmful is a(n) _____ (*untruth*). Only certain kinds of stress are harmful.

4. I have a(n) _____ (*theory*) that people who are happy are usually healthy, too.

5. Last year, scientists _____ (*proposed*) several new theories about health.

6. Judy has a(n) _____ (*deep*) interest in becoming a musician.

7. As children grow, they try to gain more _____ (*independence*), especially once they can walk and talk.

8. The university _____ (*established*) a policy to provide student aid to those with low incomes, but good grades.

9. There is a clear _____ (*connection*) between smoking and cancer.

10. Cutting calories is an important _____ (*element*) in extending longevity.

Vocabulary in Context

Read the following sentences. Complete each sentence with the correct word from the box. Use each word only once.

demands *(n.)*	generate *(v.)*	maintain *(v.)*	reversed *(v.)*
enhance *(v.)*	key *(adj.)*	moderately *(adv.)*	ties *(n.)*
extension *(n.)*	landmark *(adj.)*		

1. Anna exercises _____. She walks or rides her bike for 30 minutes every day.

2. Small children make many _____ on their parents because they are very dependent on their mother and father.

3. Keeping to a healthy diet is a(n) _____ factor to having a long life.

4. You can _____ your college application and increase your chances of getting a scholarship by getting good grades and doing volunteer work in the community.

5. The _____ between parents and children are very strong.

6. If we want to _____ more income, we need to get higher-paying jobs.

7. To park, the driver first drove forward, then _____ to fit his car into the parking space.

8. The head of the company made a(n) _____ decision when he made the employees co-owners of the firm. No company head had ever done that before.

9. You can _____ your good health by exercising regularly, eating well, and getting the right amount of sleep every night.

10. When Sid lost his job, he asked the bank for a one-year _____ on his loan because he needed more time to pay it back.

Reading Skill

Using Headings to Create a Chart

Readings often have headings. Headings introduce new ideas or topics. They also introduce details. Using headings to make a chart can help you understand and remember the most important information from the reading.

Read the passage again. Then complete the following chart.

Factors Affecting Longevity		
_____		Changeable
	_____	_____
1. gender	1.	1. Expert:
2.	2.	2. Autonomy Expert: Toni Antonucci
3.	3. Eat breakfast regularly.	3. Expert:
	4.	4. Expert:
	5.	5. Expert: Unnamed researchers
	6.	
	7.	
	The single most important lifestyle change you can make is: Source:	

What you can do:

1. _____

   _____

2. _____

   _____

Expert: _____

Information Recall

Review the information in the chart. Then answer the questions.

1. What is the difference between fixed factors and changeable factors?

   _____

   _____

2. Which factor in the first set of changeable factors is most important? Who is the expert and what was his opinion?

   _____

   _____

3. Choose two changeable factors in the second set. Briefly describe the experts' opinions for the two factors.

   _____

   _____

4. What is the expert's opinion about what you can do to live longer?

   _____

   _____

Write a brief summary of the passage. It should not be more than five sentences. Use your own words. Be sure to indent the first sentence.

Another Perspective

🎧 **Read the article and answer the questions that follow.**

CD 1
TR 13

The Real Secrets to a Longer Life

by Amy Novotney, *The Monitor*

Amy Novotney of The Monitor interviewed psychologist Howard S. Friedman, Ph.D. of the University of California, Riverside. Dr. Friedman and Dr. Leslie Martin are co-authors of the book "The Longevity Project."

Most people who live to old age do so not because they have beaten cancer, heart disease, depression, or diabetes. Instead, the long-lived avoid serious ailments altogether through a series of steps that often rely on long-lasting, meaningful connections with others, says Dr. Friedman. His and Dr. Martin's book, "The Longevity Project," is a compilation of findings from their work on an eight-decade research project examining the longevity of more than 1,500 children first studied by psychologist Lewis Terman,

10   Ph.D., in 1921. It's an attempt to answer the question of who lives longest—and why—based on personality traits, relationships, experiences and career paths.

    Ms. Novotney asked Dr. Friedman about some of the most controversial of his findings—including the idea that stress isn't necessarily all that bad for us.

Why did you choose to use Terman's study?

    In 1989, I was frustrated with the state of research about individual differences, stress,
15   health and longevity. It was clear that some people were more prone to disease, took longer to recover or died sooner, while others of the same age were able to thrive, but there was no good way to test explanations over the long term. I wanted to know who was more likely to later develop cancer or heart disease and die before their time. But how to do such a study? Most troublingly, I'd be long dead before the results came in.
20   Then one day it struck me: Build upon the Terman data, extending a study that began in 1921. We planned to spend a year, but more than two decades later, I am still at it.

What surprised you the most about his findings?

    We were amazed to uncover lots of evidence that it is not random who will become ill. Rather, there are large differences in susceptibility to injury and disease. Some of these are a function of personality. Others are tied to social relations, including
25   marriage, family, friendship, and religious observance. Most eye-opening is our finding that the risk factors and protective shields bunch together in patterns.

Does stress negatively affect longevity?

    There is a terrible misunderstanding about stress. Chronic physiological disturbance is not the same thing as hard work, social challenges, or demanding careers. People are being given rotten advice to slow down, take it easy, stop worrying, and retire to
30   Florida. The Longevity Project discovered that those who worked the hardest lived the longest. The responsible and successful achievers thrived in every way, especially if they were dedicated to things and people beyond themselves.

Questions for Another Perspective

1. What did Dr. Lewis Terman do?

_____

_____

2. a. Who did Dr. Friedman and Dr. Martin decide to study?

_____

_____

b. Why did they choose these particular research subjects?

_____

_____

3. What is one of the controversial findings from Dr. Friedman's and Dr. Martin's research?

_____

_____

4. How do Dr. Friedman and Dr. Martin disagree with the general description of stress?

_____

_____

Topics for Discussion and Writing

1. In a small group, discuss the factors that might shorten a person's life expectancy, for example, health factors such as smoking or a poor diet, and psychosocial factors such as stress or job satisfaction. For each of the factors your group selects, discuss measures that might be taken to change these factors in people's lives to help them live longer, healthier lives.

2. Work with a partner. Make a list of the steps you can take to increase your life expectancy. Share your list with your classmates.

3. Refer to the "Global Life Expectancy at Birth" map on page 134. Choose a country other than your own from the map. Write a composition about the life expectancy in this country. Do an online search for the reasons for this country's high or low life expectancy. Present your information to the class.

4. Write in your journal. How long would you like to live? Explain your answer.

5. Study the life expectancy chart; then answer the questions that follow.

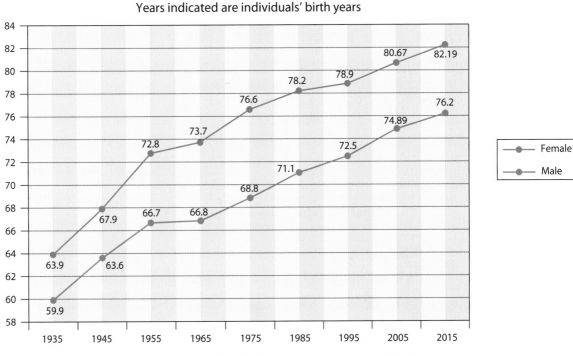

Life Expectancy in the United States
Years indicated are individuals' birth years

a. 1. About how long can a female born in 2015 expect to live?

   _____

   2. About how long can a male born in 2015 expect to live?

   _____

b. In what year was there the greatest difference in life expectancy between males and females?

   _____

c. In what decade did life expectancy for females make the greatest gain?
   1. Between 1935 and 1945
   2. Between 1945 and 1955
   3. Between 1955 and 1965
   4. Between 1975 and 1985

d. How many years did females gain?

_____

e. In what decade did life expectancy for males make the greatest gain?
   1. Between 1935 and 1945
   2. Between 1945 and 1955
   3. Between 1955 and 1965
   4. Between 1975 and 1985

f. How many years did males gain?

_____

g. In general terms, speculate on what could account for this dramatic increase in life expectancy for *both* sexes in the particular decade?

_____

_____

6. Study the map. Then answer the questions that follow.

Global Life Expectancy at Birth in 2015

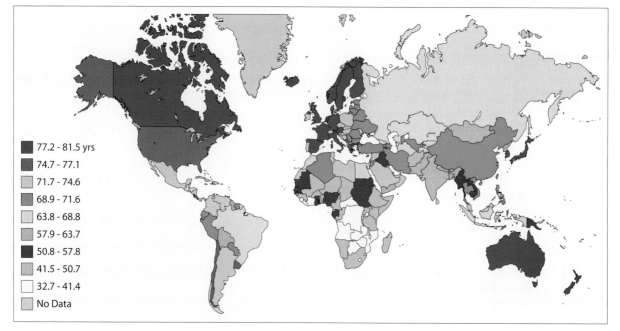

77.2 - 81.5 yrs
74.7 - 77.1
71.7 - 74.6
68.9 - 71.6
63.8 - 68.8
57.9 - 63.7
50.8 - 57.8
41.5 - 50.7
32.7 - 41.4
No Data

a. What does this map illustrate?

_____

b. Locate your country on the map. What is the average life expectancy?

_____

c. What is the highest life expectancy in the world? Where is it?

_____

d. What is the lowest life expectancy in the world? Where is it?

_____

e. What are some factors that might account for such a range in life expectancy throughout the world, i.e. from 32.7 to 81.5?

_____

_____

Critical Thinking

1. Researchers have shown that "in laboratory animals, a 40 percent calorie reduction leads to a 50 percent extension in longevity." Why do you think that eating less had such a dramatic positive effect on the animals' longevity? How much of an extension in longevity do you think humans might gain if they cut calories? How much could they cut?

2. Why do you think volunteer work increases a woman's longevity? Think about some reasons and discuss these with your classmates.

3. According to the first passages, clerical workers suffered twice as many heart attacks as homemakers (p. 118, lines 59–60.) How are clerical workers and homemakers similar? Why do you think clerical workers suffer twice as many heart attacks as homemakers?

4. How is the information in the second reading different from the information in the first reading? What does the information in the second reading add to the information in the first reading?

5. What was Patricia Skalka's purpose in writing her article? What do you think she was hoping to accomplish by writing it?

Crossword Puzzle

Review the words in the box below. Then read the clues on the next page. Write the words in the correct spaces in the puzzle.

autonomy	extension	hostility	links	mortality
coronary	factors	hypothesis	locales	profound
demands	fallacies	ingredients	maintain	say
determine	fixed	key	moderately	ties
enhance	generate	landmark		

Crossword Puzzle Clues

ACROSS CLUES

2. Happy people generally have many _____, or relationships, with others.

7. Some _____, or areas, seem to support longevity better than others.

9. We can _____ our chances of a healthy life by following guidelines, such as not smoking.

13. What are the most important _____ for a long, healthy life?

14. Research helps doctors _____ how to advise patients on ways to live longer, healthier lives.

16. _____ disease is one of the major causes of death in the United States.

18. One way to _____ your health is to have a strong circle of friends.

19. Feelings of _____, or anger, can shorten our lives.

20. There are many _____ about living longer, but there are many facts as well.

22. You have _____ when you have control over decisions in your life.

23. Researchers discovered _____ between longevity and the psychological aspects of human life.

DOWN CLUES

1. Teachers often make considerable _____ on their students in order to help them learn.

3. If you eat and exercise _____, and do not smoke, you have a better chance of living longer.

4. Feeling independent is a(n) _____ element in successful aging.

5. Reducing calories has a more _____ effect on longevity than any other lifestyle change.

6. Three _____ are unchangeable, but many more are elements that we have control over.

8. A(n) _____ is a theory that needs to be tested through research.

10. The _____ factors relating to longevity are gender, race, and heredity.

11. Research has shown that reducing calories can lead to a(n) _____ in longevity.

12. Scientists need to _____ more research to learn how we can live longer, healthier lives.

15. The _____ rate in developed countries is lower than the death rate in less developed countries.

17. The research on 7,000 adults in California was a(n) _____ study about longevity.

21. Having a(n) _____ means being able to make decisions for yourself.

Issues in Health

1. Do you think people have the right to end their own lives if they are critically ill and there's no hope of recovery?

2. Would you donate your organs so that they can be given to someone in need after you die?

3. Do you think that eating special foods can replace taking medicine for some illnesses?

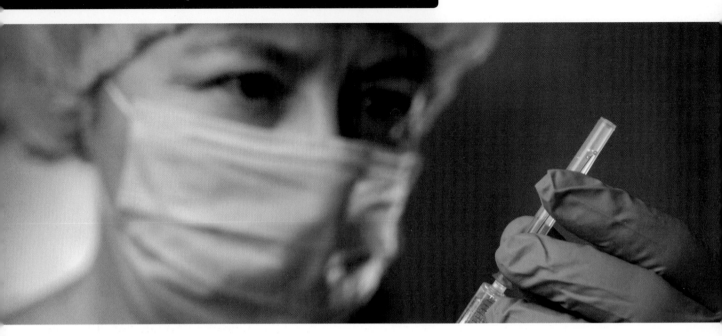

Prereading

1. What is assisted suicide? Is assisted suicide legal in your culture?

2. This chapter presents a variety of perspectives on assisted suicide. Work with a partner or in a small group. Use the chart below to make a list of different people who might have different viewpoints on assisted suicide. When you are finished, compare your list with your classmates' lists.

Person	Possible Viewpoint
a family member	

3. Work in a small group. What are some reasons a person would choose assisted suicide?

Reading

🎧 **Read the passages carefully. Then complete the exercises that follow.**

CD 1
TR 14

Assisted Suicide: Multiple Perspectives

The issue of assisted suicide is controversial. Members of the medical community often do not agree on this issue. Here, two prominent, experienced physicians, from the United States and from Great Britain, discuss their very dissimilar beliefs.

Matters of Life and Death
by Dr. Francis Moore, *National Academy of Sciences*

In his book, A Miracle and a Privilege, *Dr. Francis Moore, 81, of Harvard Medical School,*
5 *discusses a lifetime of grappling with the issue of when to help a patient die. Here is an excerpt:*

Doctors of our generation are not newcomers to this question. Going back to my internship days, I can remember many patients in pain, sometimes in a coma or delirious, with late, hopeless cancer. For many of them, we wrote an order for heavy
10 medication—morphine[1] by the clock. This was not talked about openly and little was written about it. It was essential, not controversial.

The best way to bring the problem into focus is to describe two patients whom I cared for. The first, formerly a nurse, had sustained a fractured pelvis in an automobile accident. A few days later her lungs seemed to fill up; her urine stopped; her heart developed
15 dangerous rhythm disturbances. So there she was: in a coma, on dialysis, on a breathing machine, her heartbeat maintained with an electrical device. One day after rounds, my secretary said the husband and son of the patient wanted to see me. They told me their wife and mother was obviously going to die; she was a nurse and had told her family that she never wanted this kind of terrible death, being maintained by machines. I told
20 them that while I respected their view, there was nothing intrinsically lethal about her situation. The kidney failure she had was just the kind for which the artificial kidney was most effective. While possibly a bit reassured, they were disappointed. Here was the head surgeon, seemingly determined to keep everybody alive, no matter what.

When patients start to get very sick, they often seem to fall apart all at once. The reverse
25 is also true. Within a few days, the patient's pacemaker could be removed, and she awoke from her coma. About six months later I was again in my office. The door opened and in walked a gloriously fit woman. After some cheery words of appreciation, the father and son asked to speak to me alone. As soon as the door closed, both men became quite tearful. All that came out was, "We want you to know how wrong we were."

---

[1] **Morphine** is a powerful drug used to relieve severe pain. It can cause death in large doses (amounts).

30   The second patient was an 85-year-old lady whose hair caught fire while she was smoking. She arrived with a deep burn; I knew it would surely be fatal. As a remarkable coincidence, there was a seminar going on at the time in medical ethics, given by the wife of an official of our university. She asked me if I had any sort of ethical problem I could bring up for discussion. I described the case and asked the

35   students their opinion. After the discussion, I made a remark that was, in retrospect, a serious mistake. I said, "I'll take the word back to the nurses about her and we will talk about it some more before we decide." The instructor and the students were shocked: "You mean this is a real patient?" The teacher of ethics was not accustomed to being challenged by reality. In any event, I went back and met with the nurses. A

40   day or two later, when she was making no progress and was suffering terribly, we began to back off treatment. When she complained of pain, we gave her plenty of morphine. A great plenty. Soon she died quietly and not in pain.

As a reasonable physician, you had better move ahead and do what you would want done for you. And don't discuss it with the world first. There is a lesson here

45   for everybody. Assisting people to leave this life requires strong judgment and long experience to avoid its misuse.

The Lure of Assisted Dying
by Dr. Trevor Stammers, *The Spectator*

Dr. Trevor Stammers, FRCGP (Fellow of the Royal College of General Practitioners), was a family doctor for 27 years and is now a bioethicist at St. Mary's University, Twickenham. "Doctors are not tireless saints. And the ability to deliver both life and death is intoxicating,"

50   *believes Dr. Stammers. Here are his thoughts on assisted suicide.*

'I want to die. Please help me.' It was 2 a.m. in the good old days when patients had 24-hour cover by their own GPs (general practitioners). I knew Martin well. His bladder cancer had been diagnosed the year before, but more recently it had spread and he had run out of effective treatments. Martin had borne his illness with stoicism

55   so far but on this night he was in terrible pain.

He asked to die more than once, and each time his request scared me, but not for any obvious reason. What alarmed me about Martin's death wish, both at the time and now looking back on it, is that had it been legal to kill him, I might well have done it. I would have helped him die, not through compassion but because it would

60   have been easier: a way out for me as well as him.

The Marris Assisted Dying Bill[2] wants to legalize physician-assisted suicide and though I have witnessed enough suffering and death to understand why, I am totally convinced that we should not. Marris insists that assisted dying will only be for the terminally ill, but I have my doubts. Every state that has introduced assisted

---

[2] The **Marris Assisted Dying Bill** was introduced into British Parliament to enable competent adults who are terminally ill to choose to be provided with medically supervised assistance to end their own life. In September, 2015, Parliament voted against the bill.

suicide for the terminally ill has ended up using it for the mentally ill or just those tired of life.

Supporters of assisted dying assume that doctors are saints, with endless reserves of compassion. They assume a doctor always acts in a patient's best interests. But even the most dedicated doctors become tired and numb to suffering. Death itself and certainly the desire for it doesn't keep regular hours, and I was dog-tired when I arrived at Martin's bedside. I couldn't honestly tell you that I wouldn't have taken the line of least resistance in order to get back to sleep as quickly as possible. Martin lived alone and was diagnosed as terminally ill. No one would have turned a hair if the law had allowed it.

Recently I attended a small gathering of doctors in favor of assisted dying and, as I listened to them talk, I realized they all seemed scarily eager to 'do their first one.' It's not that they were a callous bunch so much that the idea of being able to deliver both life and death was intoxicating. The evidence from the Netherlands and from Belgium is that doctors do get mesmerized by it. Others just become inured, or accustomed, to it, which is equally dangerous. An inured physician stops asking questions. He becomes more inclined to just get on with the job.

I am glad the law did not allow me to grant Martin his request in the early hours. His pain turned out to be mainly from loneliness and precipitated by a bladder infection which was successfully treated. His anguish subsequently abated. Martin had a few good months after that with no recurrence of the infection, and several months later he died peacefully.

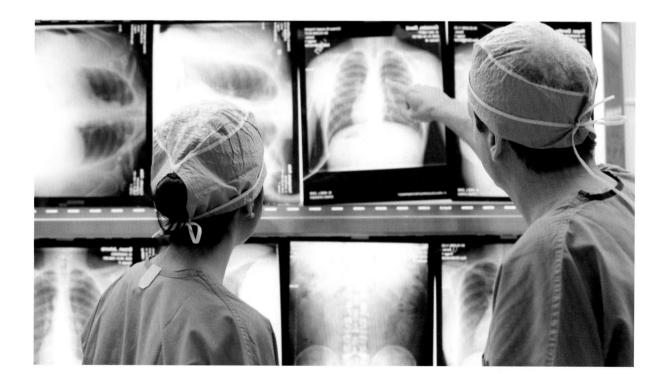

Statement Evaluation

Read the passage again. Then read the following statements. Indicate whether each statement is True (T), False (F), or an Inference (I). If a statement is false, rewrite it so that it is true. Then go back to the passage and find the information that supports your answers.

1. _____ The first patient discussed, who was formerly a nurse, died.

   _____

2. _____ The first patient's husband and son wanted the doctor to end her life.

   _____

3. _____ The instructor and students were very surprised that Dr. Moore was discussing a real patient.

   _____

4. _____ Dr. Moore gave the 85-year-old woman enough morphine so that she would die.

   _____

5. _____ Dr. Moore would probably choose assisted suicide if he should become terminally ill.

   _____

6. _____ At the time Dr. Stammers was treating Martin, assisted suicide was legal.

   _____

7. _____ Dr. Stammers worries that assisted suicide may not be used only for the terminally ill if it is legalized in Great Britain.

   _____

8. _____ Doctors sometimes do not make the best decisions for their patients.

   _____

9. _____ Doctors never become accustomed to death and dying among their patients.

   _____

10. _____ Martin eventually stopped asking Dr. Stammers to help him die.

   _____

Reading Analysis

Read each question carefully. Circle the letter or number of the correct answer, or write your answer in the space provided.

1. Read lines 1–3.

   a. **Controversial** refers to

      1. something people agree on.

      2. something people argue about.

      3. something people have to do.

   b. **Prominent** means

      1. well-known and respected.

      2. educated and experienced.

      3. well trained and skilled.

2. Read lines 4–6. An **excerpt** is

   a. an example of an issue.

   b. a part of a longer reading.

   c. an introduction to a book.

3. Read lines 7–11.

   a. **Doctors of our generation** refers to

      1. old doctors.

      2. young doctors.

      3. doctors about the same age as the author.

   b. What does **this question** refer to?

   _____

   c. **My internship days** refers to

      1. the time when the author was younger.

      2. the time in the author's recent past.

      3. the time when the author was training as a doctor.

   d. What is **morphine**?

   _____

   e. Where did you find this information?

   _____

f. How did doctors of Dr. Moore's generation use morphine?
   1. To relieve the pain of patients with very serious conditions
   2. To help patients with hopeless diseases to die
   3. Both 1 and 2

g. **Essential** means
   1. necessary.
   2. medical.
   3. expensive.

h. What was essential?
   1. Ordering heavy medication for certain patients
   2. Making sure hopelessly ill patients died
   3. Giving continuous doses of morphine

4. Read line 13.
   a. **Sustained** means
      1. suffered.
      2. treated.
      3. observed.

   b. **Fractured** means
      1. destroyed.
      2. broken.
      3. bruised.

5. Read lines 14–22.
   a. Match each of the woman's conditions with the treatment she received for them.

   _____ 1. Her lungs seemed to fill up.   a. She was given an electrical device (a pacemaker).

   _____ 2. Her urine stopped.   b. She was put on a breathing machine.

   _____ 3. Her heart developed dangerous   c. She was put on dialysis.
            rhythm disturbances.

   b. **Rounds** refers to
      1. continuous movements by the doctor.
      2. doctors' regular hospital visits to their patients.
      3. daily changes of staff in a hospital.

c. **Being maintained by machines** means
1. being carefully watched.
2. being made better.
3. being kept alive.

d. **Lethal** means
1. very serious.
2. complex.
3. deadly.

e. **There was nothing intrinsically lethal about her situation** means
1. the woman's condition would most likely not cause death.
2. the woman's condition would most likely cause death.

f. **Reassured** means
1. comforted.
2. informed.
3. respected.

6. Read lines 24–27.
   a. What does **the reverse is also true** mean?
   1. Sometimes the patient suddenly starts to get well.
   2. Sometimes the patient dies suddenly.
   3. Sometimes the patient becomes even more ill.

   b. Who was the **gloriously fit woman**?

   _____

7. Read lines 31–33.
   a. **I knew it would surely be fatal** means
   1. the doctor thought the patient would live.
   2. the doctor thought the patient would die.
   3. the doctor knew the patient would die.

   b. A **seminar** is
   1. a university course.
   2. a professional conference.
   3. a medical treatment.

   c. **Ethics** refers to
   1. issues of medical treatment.
   2. issues of right and wrong.
   3. issues of students' grades.

8. Read lines 35–42.
   a. **In retrospect** means
      1. looking at something seriously.
      2. looking sadly at something.
      3. looking back at a past situation.
   b. The instructor and her students
      1. always discussed real patients and their conditions.
      2. never discussed real patients and their conditions.
   c. **In any event** means
      1. anyway.
      2. however.
      3. moreover.
   d. **We gave her plenty of morphine. A great plenty.** These sentences mean
      1. the doctors gave the woman enough morphine to eliminate her pain.
      2. the doctors gave the woman enough morphine to improve her condition.
      3. the doctors gave the woman enough morphine to cause her death.

9. Read lines 43–46.
   a. **Don't discuss it with the world first** means
      1. don't talk about your patients at seminars.
      2. don't talk about your patients with nurses.
      3. don't talk to too many people about your patients.
   b. **Misuse** means
      1. use in a wrong way.
      2. use too much.
      3. use to kill.
   c. What is the lesson Dr. Moore wants everyone to understand?
      1. It's never easy to decide to help end a very ill person's life, but it's often necessary.
      2. Deciding whether to help end a person's life requires a lot of knowledge and experience.
      3. Many very ill patients want to end their lives, but are unable to do it on their own.

10. Read lines 49–50. **Intoxicating** means
    a. thrilling.
    b. serious.
    c. miraculous.

11. Read lines 52–55.
- a. **Diagnosed** means
  1. increased in seriousness.
  2. discussed among doctors.
  3. recognized through examination.
- b. **Stoicism** describes the attitude of a person who
  1. does not complain even though he is in a bad situation.
  2. shows that he is in a lot of pain because of his illness.
  3. has had many different treatments that were unsuccessful.

12. Read lines 57–60.
- a. **Alarmed** means
  1. changed.
  2. interested.
  3. unnerved.
- b. **Compassion** means
  1. emotion.
  2. sympathy.
  3. impatience.

13. Read lines 61–63.
- a. Briefly, what was the intention of the **Marris Assisted Dying Bill**?

   _____

- b. **To legalize** means
  1. to make lawful.
  2. to assist.
  3. to consider.
- c. **Convinced** means
  1. experienced.
  2. worried.
  3. persuaded.

14. Read lines 67–72.
- a. **Endless reserves** means
  1. countless options.
  2. continuous energy.
  3. unending supplies.
- b. **To take the line of least resistance** means
  1. to follow a line of thought.
  2. to use the least difficult treatment.
  3. to make the easiest decision.

15. Read lines 76–80.

    a. **Callous** means

        1. unfeeling.

        2. angry.

        3. unprofessional.

    b. In these sentences, a synonym for **inured** is

    _____

16. What is the main idea of the passage?

    a. Assisted suicide is not a new topic for doctors, and they have been struggling with this very controversial issue for many years.

    b. Both family members and doctors sometimes make the wrong decision regarding assisted suicide for the very ill.

    c. Assisted suicide is a very difficult and controversial decision, but it is necessary in some situations.

Vocabulary Skills

PART 1

Recognizing Word Forms

In English, the verb and noun forms of some words are the same, for example, *progress (n.)*, *progress (v.)*.

Complete each sentence with the correct form of the word on the left. Then circle *(v.)* if you are using a verb or *(n.)* if you are using a noun. Use the correct form of the verb in either the affirmative or the negative. The nouns may be singular or plural.

challenge

    1. Deciding the issue of helping a patient die is a _____ to doctors.
                                                  (n., v.)

        Dr. Moore _____ the students at the seminar to give their
                        (n., v.)

        opinion on this ethical problem.

focus   **2.** The _____ of the seminar was an ethical discussion of assisted
                              (n., v.)

suicide. The doctor _____ on two different patients in similar
                                           (n., v.)

situations.

remark   **3.** When Dr. Moore _____ that the patient they were discussing at
                                     (n., v.)

the seminar was a real person, the students were in disbelief. They were shocked

by all his _____ .
                (n., v.)

doubt   **4.** I _____ that this patient is very ill. In fact, I am sure he is quite
                        (n., v.)

sick. If you have a(n) _____ about the seriousness of his
                                (n., v.)

illness, please speak to his doctor.

request   **5.** You should not have given the patient that medication. The doctor

_____ it for her. In the future, make sure you read all the
        (n., v.)

doctor's _____ on the patient's information chart before you
                  (n., v.)

give her any medication.

PART 2

Phrasal Verbs

A phrasal verb is a verb plus an adverb, a preposition, or both. Phrasal verbs have a different meaning from the original verb. *Grapple with, care for, fill up, bring up, back off, get on with, look back on, get back to,* and *run out of* are common phrasal verbs.

First, match each phrasal verb with the correct meaning. Then complete each sentence with the correct phrasal verb. Use the past tense if necessary, and use each phrasal verb only once.

_____ 1. back off   a. look after

_____ 2. bring up   b. proceed with

_____ 3. care for   c. reduce

_____ 4. fill up   d. reflect on

_____ 5. get back to   e. retain fluid

_____ 6. get on with   f. return to

_____ 7. grapple with   g. struggle with

_____ 8. look back on   h. suggest

_____ 9. run out of   i. use up

1. The instructor at the seminar asked Dr. Moore to _____ a type of ethical problem to discuss with the students.

2. Many doctors _____ the controversial issue of when to help a patient die.

3. Dr. Moore believes that once the decision about assisted suicide has been made, it is the

physician's responsibility to _____ that decision on his own.

4. It's often difficult for a family to _____ their extremely ill loved one at home.

5. In very serious cases, such as end-stage cancer, doctors _____ options for treating a patient.

6. The patient's lungs began to _____ , resulting from the serious injury caused by her car accident.

7. After discussing a patient's case with nurses and other specialists, the doctor needed to

_____ the job of taking care of her patient.

8. Because the fatally injured woman was suffering so terribly, Dr. Moore decided to

_____ treatment and give her pain medication instead.

9. When Dr. Stammer and others _____ their previous terminal patients, they often decide that they did their best at the time.

Vocabulary in Context

Read the following sentences. Complete each sentence with the correct word from the box. Use each word only once.

controversial *(adj.)*	fatal *(adj.)*	misuse *(n.)*	retrospect *(n.)*
essential *(adj.)*	generation *(n.)*	reassured *(adj.)*	sustained *(v.)*
ethics *(n.)*	maintained *(v.)*		

1. Marta was hurt in a car accident. Fortunately, her injuries were not _____ . She only had some small cuts.

2. Lee successfully _____ his high grades by doing all his homework and studying for every exam.

3. My sister and I felt very _____ when the prominent surgeon told us that our grandfather's surgery had gone very well and he would recover quickly.

4. In order to stay healthy, we must avoid the _____ of any medications our doctor prescribes for us.

5. When we make important decisions in our lives, we need to consider the _____ of a situation, what is right and what is wrong.

6. Considering all our choices is a(n) _____ part of making wise decisions.

7. Geraldo _____ a broken arm during a football game. He can't play for two months.

8. Every _____ seems to prefer a different kind of music. For example, my grandparents enjoy classical music, while my friends and I prefer hip hop.

9. The death penalty is a very _____ issue. People for and against it have strong reasons for their opinions.

10. Tom bought an expensive new car. However, in _____ , he feels he should not have spent so much money on it.

Reading Skill

Read the passage again. Then complete the following graphic organizer. Be sure to indicate whether each doctor opposes or does not oppose assisted suicide.

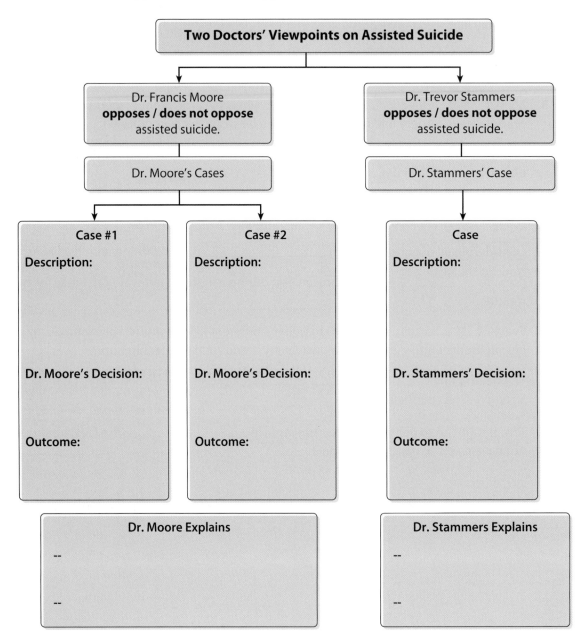

Two Doctors' Viewpoints on Assisted Suicide

Dr. Francis Moore
opposes / does not oppose
assisted suicide.

Dr. Trevor Stammers
opposes / does not oppose
assisted suicide.

Dr. Moore's Cases

Dr. Stammers' Case

Case #1

Description:

Dr. Moore's Decision:

Outcome:

Case #2

Description:

Dr. Moore's Decision:

Outcome:

Case

Description:

Dr. Stammers' Decision:

Outcome:

Dr. Moore Explains

--

--

Dr. Stammers Explains

--

--

Information Recall

Review the information in the graphic organizer. Then answer the questions.

1. Briefly describe how Dr. Moore made his decision regarding his first patient, and what happened to the first patient.

   _____

   _____

2. Briefly describe how Dr. Moore made his decision regarding his second patient, and what happened to the second patient.

   _____

   _____

3. Briefly describe how Dr. Stammers made his decision regarding his patient, and what happened to the patient.

   _____

   _____

4. How do Dr. Moore's and Dr. Stammers' views on assisted suicide differ?

   _____

   _____

5. What do both doctors believe is a potential danger of legal assisted suicide?

   _____

   _____

Writing a Summary

When writing a summary, it is important to include only main ideas. Use your own words; do not copy from the reading.

Write a brief summary of the passage. It should not be more than five sentences. Use your own words. Be sure to indent the first sentence.

Another Perspective

🎧 **Read the article and answer the questions that follow.**

CD 1
TR 15

Should doctors be allowed to help terminally ill patients commit suicide?

by Derek Humphry and Daniel Callahan, *Health*

YES

It would be a great comfort to people who face terminal illness to know they could get help to die if their suffering became unbearable. All pain cannot be
5 controlled, and it's arrogant for anybody to say that it can. Quality of life decisions are the sole right of the individual.

It's nonsense to say that death shouldn't be part of a doctor's job—it already is. We
10 all die. Death is a part of medicine. One of

NO

If it's a question of someone's wanting the right to die, I say jump off a building. But as soon as you bring in somebody else to help you, it changes the equation. Suicide is legally available to people in this country. Just don't ask a doctor to help you do it. That would violate the traditions of medicine and raise doubts about the role of the physician.

a doctor's jobs is to write death certificates. So this idea of the doctor as superhealer is a load of nonsense. The fact is that it's not so easy to commit suicide on your own.

15 It's very hard for decent citizens to get deadly drugs. Even if they do, there's the fear that the drugs won't work. There are hundreds of dying people who couldn't lift their hand to their mouth

20 with a cup of coffee, let alone a cup of drugs. They need assistance.

Of course, people who are depressed or who feel they are a weight on their families should be counseled and

25 helped to live. But you have to separate those instances from people who are dying, whose bodies are giving up on them. If you think there is a cure around the corner for your malady,

30 then please wait for it. That is your choice. But sometimes a person realizes that her life is coming to an end, as in the case of my wife, whose doctor said, "There is nothing else we can do."

35 We're not talking about cases in which a depressed person will come to a doctor and ask to be killed. Under the law the Hemlock Society is trying to get passed, the doctor must say *no*

40 to depressed people. A candidate for assisted suicide has to be irreversibly, terminally, hopelessly ill and judged to be so by two doctors.

Derek Humphry is the founder of the
45 *Hemlock Society and author of* Final Exit, *a book advising terminally ill people on how to commit suicide.*

One of my worries is that people will be manipulated by a doctor's suggesting suicide. A lot of seriously ill people already feel they're a burden because they're costing their families money. It would be easy for a family to insinuate, "While we love you, Grandmother, and we're willing to spend all our money and not send the kids to college, wouldn't it be better if . . . ?" There is no coercion there, but you build on somebody's guilt. We'd have a whole new class of people considering suicide who hadn't thought about it before.

Then, too, I don't believe that you could successfully regulate this practice. The relationship between the doctor and the patient begins in confidentiality. If they decide together that they don't want anybody to know, there is no way the government can regulate it. The presumption is that physicians would only be helping people commit suicide after everything else had failed to end their suffering. But a lot of people won't want to be that far along. None of the proposed regulations takes into account a person who is not suffering now, but who says, "I don't want to suffer in the future. Let me commit suicide now." I can imagine a doctor who would say, "Yes, we're going to make sure that you don't have to suffer at all."

Daniel Callahan is a bioethicist and director of the Hastings Center, a medical ethics think tank in Briarcliff Manor, New York.

Questions for Another Perspective

1. Describe Derek Humphry's position on doctor-assisted suicide for
   a. terminally ill people

   _____

   b. depressed people

   _____

2. What do you think happened to Derek Humphry's wife? Explain your answer.

   _____

   _____

3. Describe Daniel Callahan's position on doctor-assisted suicide for terminally ill people.

   _____

   _____

4. What are some reasons that Daniel Callahan gives for his opinion?

   _____

   _____

Topics for Discussion and Writing

1. In the United States, some people write a "living will" before their death. A "living will" can prevent doctors from prolonging a person's life if he or she becomes seriously ill. For example, the person may not want to be resuscitated if he or she stops breathing, or placed on a respirator or feeding tube if he or she cannot breathe or eat on his or her own. Would you want to write a "living will"? If not, why not? If so, under what conditions would you want to be allowed to die naturally?

2. Discuss the following questions with your classmates: What did the husband and the son of the former nurse want the doctor to do? Why were they disappointed? When the father and son revisited him, Dr. Moore states that both men became quite tearful. Why do you think they reacted this way?

3. What is your opinion on doctor-assisted suicide? Should it be legal? Should it be banned? Give reasons for your opinion.

4. Write in your journal. If someone you loved were terminally ill and wanted his or her doctor to perform an assisted suicide, would you approve? Would you encourage the doctor to agree to assist in the suicide? Explain your answer.

Critical Thinking

1. Work with one or two classmates. Review the different perspectives given by the authors in this chapter, and review your chart in the Prereading on page 140. Whose perspectives were included? Whose perspectives were omitted? What perspectives might these excluded people have? Make a list of these people and their possible perspectives, and discuss them with the class.

2. In his later years, Dr. Francis Moore suffered from a very serious type of heart disease. After years of illness, he took his own life at the age of 88. What do you think this act tells us about the kind of person Dr. Moore was? Why do you think this?

3. Work in groups of three or four students. Discuss the following case.

   Brian is a 40-year-old father of two young children. He was recently involved in a serious car accident and was critically injured. The doctors have declared him "brain dead," which means that his brain does not show any mental activity at all. He is being kept alive on a feeding tube and a respirator that breathes for him because he cannot breathe on his own. The doctors do not believe he will ever improve. However, he could be kept alive, but unconscious, on the machines indefinitely. The family must make an extremely difficult decision: Should they continue to keep Brian on these machines in the hospital, which is costing thousands of dollars a day, or should they allow him to die? Although Brian's family does not have a lot of money, they love him very much. What do you think they should do? What might be the consequences of this decision?
   a. As a class, form a medical ethics committee. Discuss each group's decision and the possible consequences. Then decide what you think Brian's family should do.
   b. Think about how you came to your decision. What factors or values influenced your decision?

4. In the first readings and in the Another Perspective article, Dr. Moore and Derek Humphry express one viewpoint on assisted suicide, while Dr. Stammers and Daniel Callahan voice an opposite opinion. What are their opinions? Which two people do you think offer the stronger opinion? Explain your reasons for your answer.

Crossword Puzzle

Review the words in the box below. Then read the clues on the next page. Write the words in the correct spaces in the puzzle.

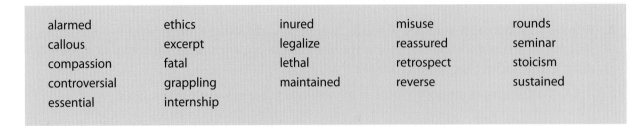

alarmed	ethics	inured	misuse	rounds
callous	excerpt	legalize	reassured	seminar
compassion	fatal	lethal	retrospect	stoicism
controversial	grappling	maintained	reverse	sustained
essential	internship			

Crossword Puzzle Clues

ACROSS CLUES

2. I thought I had made a good decision, but in _____, I realize I didn't.

7. Helping relieve a patient's pain is a(n) _____ part of caring for him.

8. A very large dose of a strong narcotic is often _____.

10. Doctors usually make their regular _____ in the hospital early in the morning.

11. What are the _____ involved in assisting a patient to die?

15. Although the man's injury didn't appear serious, it was _____ and he died within a week.

17. Many people would not want to be _____ on life-support machines to keep them alive.

18. I read a 10-page _____ from this book, and now I want to read the entire book.

20. Tom could enlist in the military, then go to college afterward, or he could do the _____.

21. After medical school, a student must serve a(n) _____ as a doctor in training.

22. The death penalty and assisted suicide are both very _____ issues.

DOWN CLUES

1. When people deliberately use a medication for the wrong purpose, they _____ the drug.

3. _____ is an important quality for doctors to have. They need to care about their patients.

4. A person who is _____ to the suffering of others often creates hard feelings.

5. Many people _____ severe injuries when their train went off the track at high speed.

6. Anna accepted her serious medical condition with _____ and rarely complained.

9. In the United States, it is up to each state to decide whether to _____ assisted suicide.

12. Most doctors are not _____. They sympathize with their patients.

13. Sara became quite _____ when her doctors told her she had cancer.

14. Doctors will never stop _____ with the issue of whether to help a patient die.

16. The sick child was _____ when his mother stayed with him in the hospital.

19. We attended a(n) _____ at the university. The topic was assisted suicide.

Prereading

1. Many people need organ transplants. For example, a person may need a kidney, a lung, or a heart. How do they get the organs they need?

2. *Illicit* means wrongful or immoral, but it does not mean illegal. How might trading in human organs be illicit, but not illegal?

3. Read the title of the article and discuss it with a partner. What do you think this reading will be about?

Reading

Read the passage carefully. Then complete the exercises that follow.

CD 1
TR 16

Organ Shortage Fuels Illicit Trade in Human Parts

by Brian Handwerk, *National Geographic*

In 2002, U.S. doctors performed 24,900 lifesaving organ transplants[1]. That's the good news. But for every person lucky enough to receive a transplant, two others are added to a waiting list that now features more than 80,000 people in the United States alone. As desperation grows, so may an illicit trade in human organs in much of the developing world. In the United States, a new person is added to the United Network for Organ Sharing (UNOS) list every 14 minutes," UNOS spokesperson Anne Paschke told *National Geographic News.* The Richmond, Virginia-based organization administers the nation's Organ Procurement and Transplantation Network (OPTN), established by the U.S. Congress in 1984.

10   In 2002, over 6,000 Americans died while waiting for organs, according to UNOS data. What would it be worth to somehow move to the top of the list? Perhaps no cost would be too high, but organs are not generally offered for sale—at least not legally. In most of the world, laws specifically ban the sale of organs. U.S. law, for example, prohibits any "valuable consideration" resulting from an organ donation. But with
15   demand so high, many have attempted to profit by selling organs such as kidneys obtained from living donors tempted to give up their "spare" organs for cash.

     In 2003, police in South Africa and in Brazil broke up an international ring trafficking in human kidneys. The racket also involved people in Israel—and possibly even further afield. Brazilian police reported that dozens of willing donors were
20   flown from that nation's destitute neighborhoods to South Africa, where transplant surgery was performed on patients, including some from Israel. Recipients may have paid as much as U.S. $100,000 for their ill-gotten organs. Donors received a fraction of that amount, but a substantial sum nonetheless to those in desperate straits.

     Though this ring is now out of business, the operation was far from unique.
25   National Geographic *Ultimate Explorer* host Lisa Ling recently traveled to India to investigate reports of a widespread trade in organs illegally harvested from that nation's poor.

---

[1]In 2015 in the United States, 30,973 organ transplants were performed. 121,678 people were on the waiting list for an organ transplant.

CHAPTER 8   Organ Shortage Fuels Illicit Trade in Human Parts   **163**

Kidney Village

Ling visited a desperate neighborhood known locally as "kidney village" because so many of its residents had illegally sold one of their kidneys. The practice is underground, but widespread enough that finding many donors was not a problem for the *Ultimate Explorer* team. "They said that they received about $800 a kidney, which for them is a year's salary," Ling told *National Geographic News*. "It's a decent amount of money to them, but of course when it runs out they can't sell more organs."

Many of those Ling met hadn't realized much lasting financial benefit as a result of their illegal kidney sales, but neither were they distressed at having undergone the potentially dangerous procedure. Having lost one kidney, donors are more at risk for any problems that could later affect their remaining kidney. Also, the transplant operations themselves can be dangerous or fatal—particularly when carried out in clandestine and illegal facilities. "We didn't meet anyone who had gotten sick as a result of selling one of their kidneys," Ling said. "The people we met were still living normal lives so they didn't have many regrets, they were surviving OK on one kidney. When you encounter folks who are so poverty-stricken, it's a gruesome option for them but it is an option. It certainly raises a lot of ethical questions."

Such practices in the developing world have led to "transplant tourism," in which patients travel from wealthier countries without a black market organ trade to parts of the world where both an organ and operation can be had—for a price. With demand so high and illicit trade already underway in the developing world, might some form of compensation be tried to ease the organ shortage in industrialized nations?

Experts Urge Compassion, Not Compensation

Anne Paschke explained that UNOS is not opposed to a study of possible incentives that could be provided for postmortem donations—but even such tentative proposals would fall far short of any "for profit" organ sales. "It would take action by Congress in order to test financial incentives," Paschke said. "We would support legislation that would allow pilot projects, a very careful testing of some type of financial incentives. We just don't know if it would have a positive or a negative impact."

Some individuals have suggested that more overt compensation could financially benefit donors while physically benefiting thousands in urgent need of transplants. The argument also maintains that a regulated trade would be preferable to existing black market organ dealings, which can be exploitative and unsafe. Yet such proposals have found little popular acceptance in medical and bioethics circles, where most fear the exploitation of the poor and foresee the first steps on a slippery slope that leads to a dehumanizing trade in bodies and body parts. "I don't think that I've ever seen anyone speak representing an organization that would support such a system," Paschke said.

So how to make more organs available to waiting patients worldwide? Paschke noted that UNOS is focused on utilizing the organs that *are* donated as efficiently as possible by streamlining the process that gets them from a deceased donor to a suitable recipient. Another critical goal is increasing the number of voluntary donors—which has remained relatively flat even as the waiting list has grown. The effort relies not on compensation but on compassion.

70 "What kind of message motivates people to become donors? Most will say, 'Yeah, donation is a good thing,' but that doesn't mean that they've made a decision for themselves or had a conversation with their families," Paschke said. "Our latest research shows that people are inspired when they see a real person, the story of a person who's been helped, so we're trying to focus on individuals, on the real people

75 who are on the list." Meanwhile, despite such efforts, the real people on the list must deal with the very real fear that they may not get the organ they need in time.

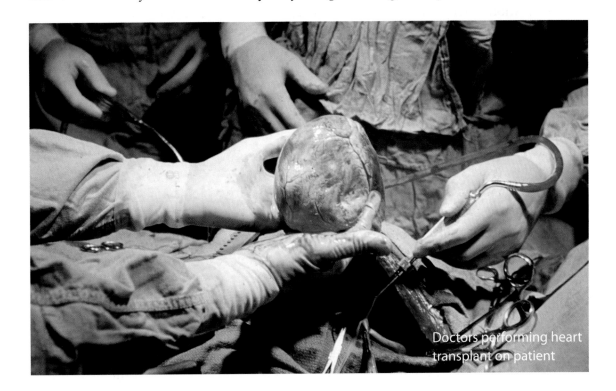

Doctors performing heart transplant on patient

Statement Evaluation

Read the passage again. Then read the following statements. Indicate whether each statement is True (T), False (F), or an Inference (I). If a statement is false, rewrite it so that it is true. Then go back to the passage and find the information that supports your answers.

1. _____ Far more people are on the waiting list for organ transplants than there are organs available.

2. _____ It is only possible to obtain an organ legally.

_____

3. _____ Some countries do not have laws prohibiting the sale of organs.

_____

4. _____ Some people become rich by selling their organs.

_____

5. _____ Most people who sell their organs are poor.

_____

6. _____ Illegally buying and selling organs can be a very profitable business.

_____

7. _____ Transplant operations are always safe.

_____

8. _____ More people might be donors if they were paid for donating their organs.

_____

9. _____ The number of voluntary donors has not been increasing over time.

_____

10. _____ Most people agree that organ donation is a good idea.

_____

Reading Analysis

Read each question carefully. Circle the letter or number of the correct answer, or write your answer in the space provided.

1. Read lines 1–5.
   a. **Performed** means
      1. attended.
      2. observed.
      3. completed.

b. **Desperation** describes
   1. an angry situation.
   2. a very strong need.
   3. an extreme fear.

2. Read lines 7–9.
   a. **Administer** means
      1. create.
      2. notice.
      3. supervise.
   b. **Procurement** means
      1. safety.
      2. acquisition.
      3. calculation.

3. Read lines 13–16.
   a. **Ban** means
      1. observe.
      2. determine.
      3. forbid.
   b. Which word in these sentences is a synonym for **ban**?

      _____

   c. **Donors** are
      1. the people whose organs are transplanted.
      2. the people who need and get organs.
   d. **Tempted** means
      1. motivated.
      2. ordered.
      3. frightened.
   e. **Spare** means
      1. new.
      2. extra.
      3. healthy.

4. Read lines 17–21.
   a. **Trafficking** means
      1. transporting.
      2. illegally trading.
      3. selling internationally.
   b. **Racket** means
      1. a business that takes advantage of people.
      2. a business that crosses international borders.
      3. a business that takes people to another country.

c. The racket involved
   1. taking poor people from Israel and giving them organs taken from South Africans.
   2. taking poor people from South Africa to remove their organs and give them to Brazilians.
   3. taking poor people from Brazil to South Africa to remove organs and give them to wealthy people who needed them.

5. Read lines 21–23.
   a. **Recipients** are
      1. the people whose organs are transplanted.
      2. the people who need and get organs.
   b. **Ill-gotten** organs means
      1. the organs were obtained improperly or illicitly.
      2. the organs obtained were for ill people.
      3. the organs obtained were from ill people.
   c. **Fraction** means
      1. a fair share.
      2. a small portion.
      3. an equal share.
   d. **Substantial** means
      1. significant.
      2. minimal.
      3. maximum.
   e. **Desperate straits** means
      1. a very poor neighborhood.
      2. a hospital in a developing country.
      3. a very difficult situation.

6. Read lines 29–31. **Underground** means
   a. very low.
   b. secretive.
   c. expensive.

7. Read lines 34–39.
   a. **Lasting** means
      1. knowing.
      2. continuing.
      3. increasing.

b. **Potentially** means
1. unfairly.
2. certainly.
3. possibly.

c. **Fatal** means
1. deadly.
2. harmful.
3. illegal.

d. **Clandestine** means
1. dirty.
2. secret.
3. dangerous.

8. Read lines 40–43.
a. **Regrets** are things
1. you wish you hadn't done.
2. you are frightened by.
3. you would like to do again.

b. **Poverty-stricken** means
1. unhealthy.
2. poor.
3. healthy.

9. Read lines 44–49.
a. **Black market** means
1. an individual business.
2. an illegal business.
3. a night market.

b. **Compensation** means
1. appreciation.
2. payment.
3. health benefit.

10. Read lines 50–52. **Postmortem** means
a. after death.
b. after an operation.
c. after recovery.

11. Read lines 58–62.

    a. **Exploitative** means

        1. extreme.

        2. expensive.

        3. unfair.

    b. **Foresee** means

        1. predict.

        2. fear.

        3. remember.

12. Read lines 67–69.

    a. **Flat** means

        1. unchanged.

        2. voluntary.

        3. costly.

    b. **Compassion** means

        1. complexity.

        2. sympathy.

        3. importance.

13. What is the main idea of the passage?

    a. Many people need organ transplants, and thousands of people die before they get one because there are not enough organs available.

    b. Many more people need organ transplants than there are organs available, which has led to illegal trade in organs taken from very poor people.

    c. Many people need organ transplants, so people have been selling their organs to meet the supply because they are poverty-stricken.

Vocabulary Skills

Recognizing Word Forms

In English, the verb and noun forms of some words are the same, for example, *report (n.)*, *report (v.)*.

Complete each sentence with the correct form of the word on the left. Then circle *(v.)* if you are using a verb or *(n.)* if you are using a noun. Use the correct form of the verb in either the affirmative or the negative. The nouns may be singular or plural.

benefit
1. Some people believe that compensation for organ donation

    _____ not only the donor, but the recipient as well. The
    (n., v.)

    _____ to the donor would be financial, while to the recipient
    (n., v.)

    it would mean good health.

demand
2. _____ for organs outweighs the number of organs actually
    (n., v.)

    available. As a result, traffickers in human kidneys _____ a high
    (n., v.)

    price for the organs from desperate potential recipients.

regret
3. Many of the poverty-stricken people who sold their organs

    _____ their action because of the financial benefit. They had
    (n., v.)

    no _____ because they hadn't gotten sick as a result of selling
    (n., v.)

    one of their kidneys.

support
4. UNOS spokesperson Anne Paschke believes that most health

    organizations _____ financial compensation for organ donors
    (n., v.)

    because they feel it is unethical. It would take _____ by
    (n., v.)

    Congress in order to test financial incentives.

trade

5. Patients from wealthy countries without a black market travel to other

parts of the world where there is a _____ in organs because

(n., v.)

poor people _____ their spare organs for money they

(n., v.)

badly need.

PART 2

Antonyms

Antonyms are words with opposite meanings. For example, *profit* and *loss* are antonyms.

First, match each word with the correct meaning. Then write the antonym of the words in parentheses in the space provided. Use each word only once.

_____ 1. ban	a. considerable
_____ 2. benefit	b. gain
_____ 3. destitute	c. horrifying
_____ 4. gruesome	d. motivation
_____ 5. incentive	e. pervasive
_____ 6. potential	f. possibility
_____ 7. substantial	g. poverty-stricken
_____ 8. suitable	h. prohibit
_____ 9. unique	i. rare
_____ 10. widespread	j. satisfactory

1. The trafficking in organs from desperately poor people is a very _____ practice. (*appealing*)

2. Truly _____ people often feel they have no choice except to sell parts of their bodies for money. (*wealthy*)

3. Tomás has the _____ to become a successful doctor one day. (*inability*)

4. Some diseases, such as cholera, are still _____ throughout the world. (*restricted*)

5. Many governments _____ the sale of organs. Organs can only be donated. (*permit*)

6. Some children need a strong _____ to study hard, which is the reason many parents reward their children for getting good grades in school. (*deterrent*)

7. Kidneys and lungs are _____ organs. They are the only organs that we have in pairs. (*common*)

8. You need to wear _____ clothes when you go to your friend's wedding. (*inappropriate*)

9. A person needs to have a(n) _____ amount of money to travel to another country to buy an organ and have a transplant operation. (*insignificant*)

10. You will experience a great health _____ when you quit smoking. (*disadvantage*)

Vocabulary in Context

bans *(v.)*	compensation *(n.)*	regret *(n.)*	substantial *(adj.)*
clandestine *(adj.)*	fraction *(n.)*	spare *(adj.)*	tempted *(v.)*
compassion *(n.)*	lasting *(adj.)*		

Read the following sentences. Complete each sentence with the correct word from the box. Use each word or phrase only once.

1. Ayana treasures her _____ friendship with Yoko. They've been close friends since high school.

2. California _____ the sale of cigarettes to people under the age of 18.

3. Even though he is on a diet, Hernando was _____ to order dessert in the restaurant.

4. My father's one _____ in life is that he never completed his college education.

5. Silvia often buys used books because they cost just a(n) _____ of the price of new ones.

6. It's important for nurses to have _____ for their patients who may be scared and in pain.

7. Apartments in this city cost a(n) _____ amount of money due to their proximity to shops, museums, restaurants, and public transportation.

8. When Delroy's car got a flat tire, he was able to change it himself because he had a(n) _____ one in the trunk.

9. The company's owners were arrested due to their _____ hiring of underage workers.

10. My sister received _____ from the parents of the child who had accidently broken her window with a baseball.

Reading Skill

Understanding Bar Graphs and Line Graphs

Bar graphs and line graphs often contain important information. It's important to understand them. Bar graphs compare numbers or amounts. Line graphs chart changes over time. Both give you information about a reading.

Read the following graphs. Then answer the questions.

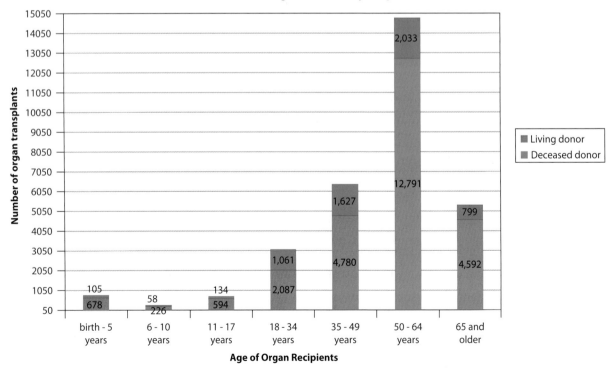

Patients who received organs in a one-year period

1. Where did the majority of donated organs come from?
   a. Living donors
   b. Deceased donors

2. Which people underwent the largest number of organ transplants?
   a. People from birth to 17 years old
   b. People from 18 to 49 years old
   c. People 50 years old and older

3. Why might so many people 50–64 years old get transplants? What do you think? Write some possible reasons.

   _____

   _____

   _____

4. Why might the number of transplants decrease among people 65 and older? What do you think? Write some possible reasons.

   _____

   _____

   _____

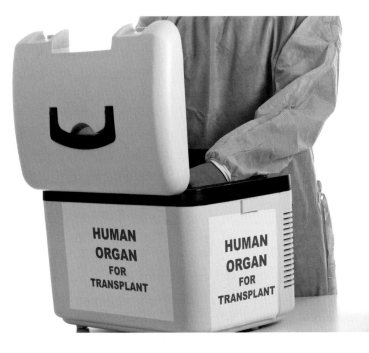

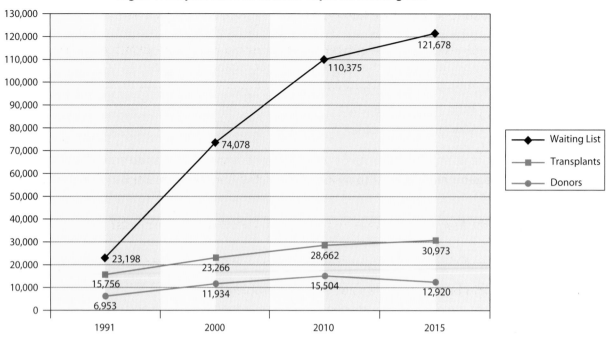

Organ Transplants, Donors, and People on Waiting List

1. What change took place in the number of donors between 2000 and 2015?
   a. The number of donors increased, then decreased.
   b. The number of donors steadily decreased over time.
   c. The number of donors steadily increased over time.

2. During which years did the number of people on the waiting list for organ transplants increase the greatest?
   a. Between 1991 and 2000
   b. Between 2000 and 2010
   c. Between 2010 and 2015

3. a. During which years did the number of organ donors decrease?
   1. Between 1991 and 2000
   2. Between 2000 and 2010
   3. Between 2010 and 2015
   b. Why does there appear to be a decline between those years?

   _____

4. What can you infer from the information in this chart? Check (√) all that apply.
   a. _____ There are more donors than transplants.
   b. _____ There are more transplants than donors.
   c. _____ Most of the people on the waiting list will get transplants.
   d. _____ Most of the people on the waiting list won't get transplants.

e. _____ The number of transplants and people waiting are increasing at the same rate.

f. _____ Many people will probably die before they are able to get a transplant.

5. How do you account for the difference between donors and transplants in any given year?

_____

Information Recall

Read the passage again, and review the information in the graphs. Then answer the questions.

1. What is the biggest problem facing people who need organ transplants?

_____

2. What might be a reasonable solution to this problem?

_____

3. What risks do living donors take when they undergo transplant surgery?

_____

Writing a Summary

When writing a summary, it is important to include only main ideas. Use your own words; do not copy from the reading.

Write a brief summary of the passage. It should not be more than five sentences. Use your own words. Be sure to indent the first sentence.

_____
_____
_____
_____
_____
_____

Another Perspective

🎧 **Read the article and answer the questions that follow.**

Saving Her Sister's Life

by Marissa Ayala, *Teen Vogue*

In 1990, Marissa Ayala's birth stirred a national debate—should families conceive one child to save another's life? In her own words, 18-year-old Marissa shares her story.

My sister, Anissa, is like my second mom. Even though she's 18 years older than me, I don't know how much closer you could be with someone. In 1988,
5   when she was 16, Anissa was diagnosed with leukemia[1]. If she didn't find a bone marrow donor, doctors said, she would die within three to five years. My parents weren't matches, so for a few years they went through every organization they could—the Life-Savers Foundation of America, the National Marrow Donor Program, City of Hope—to find donors. They couldn't find a single match. At the
10   time, the Hispanic rating for the National Marrow Donor Program was practically nonexistent, which means there were hardly any Hispanics on the list as donors. Since that's our heritage, it wasn't likely my parents would find someone who could work as a match for my sister.

Because matches are more common within families than with nonrelatives,
15   every single extended family member got tested, but none of them matched with Anissa. Finally, one of my mom's best friends said as a joke, "Mary, you should have another baby." My mom, who was 43 at the time, thought her friend was crazy. But one night my mom dreamed that God was telling her to have a baby. She took that as a sign, and in April, 1990, I was born. My parents were hoping I
20   would be a match.

When I was old enough to be tested, I turned out to be a perfect match for my sister. My family was really excited and had me donate bone marrow to her 14 months after I was born—my marrow was transplanted into hers to stimulate healthy blood-cell growth. It was a total success. I recovered perfectly—my
25   parents even have a video of me running around the same day I had my surgery. Although at first my sister had to be in an isolation room for a while so that no germs could get to her, she recovered well. She's been cancer-free for the past 18 years.

There has always been a lot of media attention surrounding our family because of
30   our situation, though. It was apparently really controversial that my parents were

---

[1]**Leukemia** is cancer of the blood cells. Blood cells are mostly formed in the body's bone marrow.

having a baby just to save their other daughter's life. I don't remember a lot of that, because I was so much younger. When I was a baby, Anissa and I were on the cover of *Time* and there was a made-for-TV movie on NBC in 1993 called *For the Love of My Child: The Anissa Ayala Story*, made about my family's experience.

35   I first started really researching my own story when I was in the seventh grade. My friends were Googling themselves and nothing came up, but when I searched for myself a lot of news articles popped up. I read negative comments from a few newspapers about how my parents were just using me to save my sister's life and weren't going to love me, and that what they did was morally wrong. It surprised me.

40   I thought, "Really? People think about my family like that?" Some of the articles said that if I hadn't been a perfect match for my sister, my parents would have disowned me. And that just wasn't the case.

I try to see both sides of the story, but I ultimately don't agree with the critics. They were probably just looking out for my safety, thinking that my parents were going

45   to have a baby solely for the purpose of saving their child. But they don't know us personally: My family loves me so much.

Every year our family takes part in the Relay for Life cancer walk and we raise money for the American Cancer Society. We try to spread the message that the need for marrow donors is great. And more importantly, that despite being diagnosed with

50   whatever type of cancer, there's a way to get through it.

There are so many ways growing up as "the baby who saved her sister" has influenced my life. I've taken it, been humbled by it, and have grown from it. But it won't be my whole life story. In the future, I plan to study either child development or psychology. My dad always tells me, "Marissa, you should do something you want to

55   do every day." I want to help people.

Marissa and Anissa Ayala.

Questions for Another Perspective

1. Marissa says, "There has always been a lot of media attention surrounding our family because of our situation."
   a. Why was there a lot of media attention?

   _____

   b. Give some examples of the media attention.

   _____

   _____

2. What negative comments did the critics make about the Ayala family? Does Marissa agree with them? Why or why not?

   _____

   _____

3. Many people know Marissa Ayala as the baby who saved her sister. How has this influenced her life today? How will this influence her in the future?

   _____

   _____

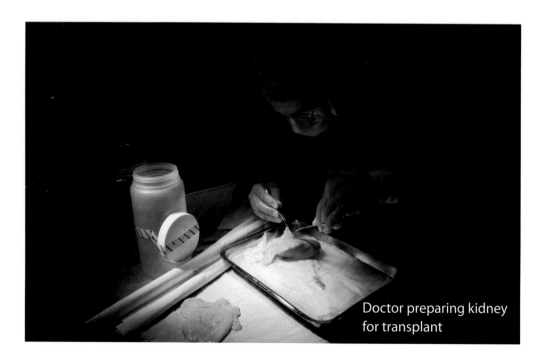

Doctor preparing kidney for transplant

Topics for Discussion and Writing

1. In a magazine survey, 47 percent of American people said they believe it is acceptable for parents to conceive a child in order to provide an organ or tissue that will save the life of another one of their children. However, 37 percent of Americans believe this is unacceptable. What do you think? Write a letter to the magazine explaining your position. Be sure to make your reasons clear.

2. What do you think is the general opinion on living-to-living organ donation (for example, the donation of a kidney or a lung lobe) in your country? Is this practice legal? Write a paragraph about living-to-living organ donation in your country. Compare it with your classmates' descriptions of living-to-living organ donation in their countries. How are the policies similar in various countries? How are they different?

3. Consider the organs in the illustration. Some organs, such as a kidney, skin, and bone marrow, can be donated while the recipient is living. Others, such as eyes, the cornea of the eye, and hearts, can be taken only after death. Which organ or organs would you be most likely to donate while you are living? After your death? Why?

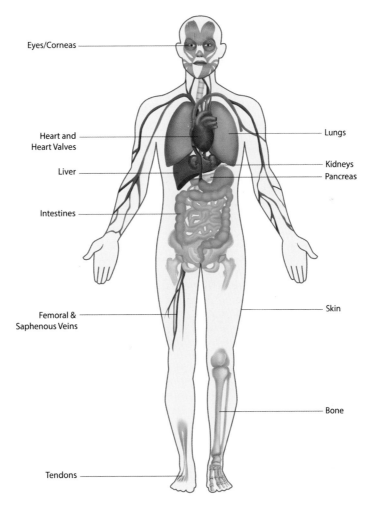

Eyes/Corneas

Heart and
Heart Valves

Lungs

Liver

Kidneys
Pancreas

Intestines

Femoral &
Saphenous Veins

Skin

Bone

Tendons

4. Conduct an in-class survey using the questions in the following chart. Record the responses in the chart. (You may use your data later if you decide to do an out-of-class survey on the same questions.) Discuss the responses in class.

Questions	Yes	No
1. Is it morally acceptable for parents to conceive a child in order to provide an organ or tissue that will save the life of another one of their children?		
2. Is it morally acceptable to remove a kidney or other nonessential organ from a living person for use in another person's body?		
3. Would you donate a kidney for transplant to a close relative who needed it?		
4. Is it ethical to ask a child under the age of 18 to give up a kidney for a transplant to a relative?		
5. If you or a close relative had a fatal disease that could possibly be cured by a transplant, which of the following would you be willing to do?		
a. Purchase the necessary organ or tissue		
b. Conceive a child to provide the necessary organ or tissue		
c. Take legal action to try to force a relative to donate		

5. Write in your journal. In the United States, people can write on the back of their driver's license if they want their organs donated, and they can specify which one(s). Would you indicate this on your driver's license? Why or why not?

Critical Thinking

1. In some places, kidneys are sold for just $800, while the recipient can pay as much as $100,000 for an organ. Why is there such a huge difference in these two amounts?

2. Why might there be a higher and higher obligation, and risk, for a living person who qualifies as a donor to a relative?

3. According to the first reading, "Another critical goal is increasing the number of voluntary donors—which has remained relatively flat even as the waiting list has grown. *The effort relies not on compensation but on compassion.*" (page 165, lines 68–69) What does that second sentence mean?

4. What is your opinion about the Ayala case? Do you approve of their decision to have another child in order to save their older daughter? Explain your opinion.

5. What is the tone of Brian Handwerk's article? Is he optimistic or pessimistic about the possibility of increasing the supply of organs for donation and decreasing the illegal sale of organs?

Crossword Puzzle

Review the words in the box below. Then read the clues on the next page. Write the words in the correct spaces in the puzzle.

ban	desperation	fraction	prohibit	suitable
benefit	destitute	gruesome	recipients	trafficking
clandestine	donors	incentive	regrets	unique
compassion	exploitative	potentially	substantial	widespread
compensation	fatal	procurement		

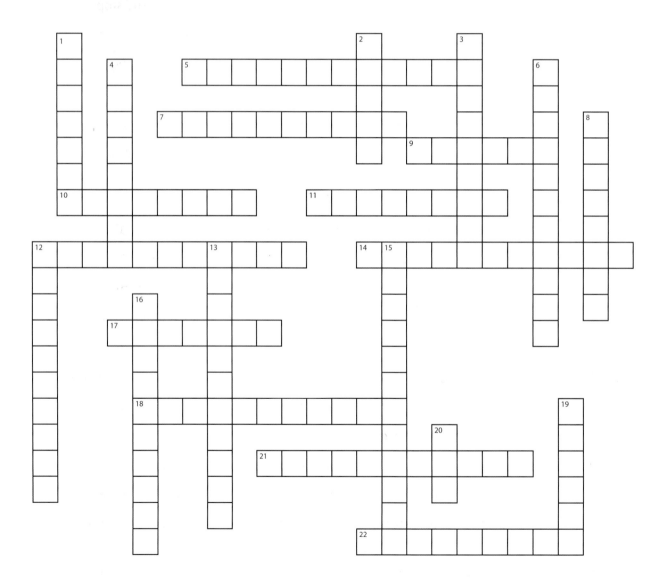

Crossword Puzzle Clues

ACROSS CLUES

5. Would money be the best type of _____ to give someone who donates an organ?

7. The business of obtaining organs from poor people is more _____ than you might think.

9. The number of _____ has not increased enough to meet the need for organs.

10. Finding a(n) _____ organ donor is a very complex process.

11. The laws in many countries _____ the sale of organs. They can only be donated.

12. Illicit practices are usually _____. It is hard to find the people responsible and stop them.

14. Some people sell one of their kidneys out of _____ for money to help their families.

17. Payment that people get for giving an organ does not _____ them for very long.

18. Most countries have organizations for the legal _____ of organs from donors.

21. The surgery involved in removing an organ is not always safe. It is _____ deadly.

22. When people are _____, they sometimes do things they would not ordinarily do.

DOWN CLUES

1. Do you have any _____ that you didn't take the job when it was offered to you?

2. Any surgery can be _____. Even a healthy person can die following an operation.

3. What type of _____ could be offered to persuade a person to donate an organ?

4. The number of organs legally available is a small _____ of the number needed for transplant.

6. For many poverty-stricken people, $800 is a(n) _____ amount of money.

8. The harvesting of organs from people, then paying them so little is a very _____ thought.

12. We must have _____ for those who need an organ transplant, and the poor, too.

13. The practice of _____ in human organs is not only illegal, it is immoral.

15. Poor people may choose to sell an organ, but it is still a very _____ practice.

16. Organ _____ are often wealthy people who can pay a lot of money to buy an organ illegally.

19. Taking advantage of poor people through organ trafficking is not _____. They are often taken advantage of in other ways, too.

20. Some people do not agree to having a(n) _____ on the buying and selling of organs.

CHAPTER 9

Writing Recipes Instead of Prescriptions: Health through Diet

Prereading

1. In what ways does our diet affect our health positively?

2. In what ways does our diet affect our health negatively?

3. Read the title of the article. How can food be more effective than prescription drugs in helping us be healthy?

Reading

🎧 **Read the passages carefully. Then complete the exercises that follow.**

Writing Recipes Instead of Prescriptions: Health through Diet

The medical community has long recognized the connection between what we eat and how healthy we are. Because of this, some medical school classes for prospective doctors focus on nutrition and diet. These classes are traditionally taught by respected physicians who have years of experience in the medical field. However, today in several medical schools in the
5 *United States, courses are being taught by trained chefs and the focus is cooking!*

Will your doctor one day prescribe food as medicine?
by Christina Farr, *KQED Science*

Is your doctor your go-to for nutritional advice? Neither is mine. And why would I expect that? According to recent polls, fewer than a quarter of doctors say they've had sufficient training to provide nutritional advice to their patients. We all know about the Hippocratic Oath[1], but how about that other thing Hippocrates said: "Let Food Be
10 Thy Medicine."

For the American medical profession to live up to that, there'd have to be more than one doctor in the country widely known for prescribing broccoli. Most medical schools aren't particularly dedicated to teaching their students about food. That's beginning to change, though, as schools like Tulane University School of Medicine in
15 New Orleans, Louisiana, start thinking differently. Would-be doctors at Tulane aren't just learning about nutrition. They're learning how to cook.

Dr. Timothy Harlan, known in the food media world as Dr. Gourmet, is also executive director at the Goldring Center for Culinary Medicine at Tulane. Harlan says the program isn't just about helping students understand nutrition. The focus is
20 on practical talk about food. Harlan wants Tulane-educated doctors to be able to teach their patients everyday skills in how to cook, what to cook, and why.

"Physicians talk about nutrition and diet all the time, but they don't talk about it in a way that communicates change to their patients," Harlan says, in a video produced by the school. The students learn to make the most of low-cost ingredients, so they
25 can cater to low-income communities. And Harlan says the school also provides cooking classes to practicing doctors and the public. These skills are sorely needed in New Orleans. In 2010, 64 percent of adults were classified as obese or overweight. That results in higher rates of diabetes, heart disease, and high blood pressure.

---

[1] The **Hippocratic Oath** is a pledge that all new doctors take, promising to uphold ethical standards. **Hippocrates** (460–370 B.C.) was a Greek physician. He is considered "The Father of Western Medicine."

"We know from the literature that when people go home and start cooking from real
ingredients for themselves that their health improves," Harlan says. "We also know that
they don't really know how to do that." Cheryl Spann took part in the community cooking
class, and says she's learned what good carbs (carbohydrates) are and how to cut back on
sugar. "My health is getting so much better now," Spann says in the school's video. "And I
do believe that when I see my primary care physician in the next month, I will no longer be
taking hypertensive medicine and I will no longer be taking diabetes medicine."

Tulane's medical school was among the first to take on a licensed chef as an
instructor. Its curriculum, developed in partnership with the College of Culinary Arts
at Johnson and Wales University, has been sold to sixteen other medical schools.

If you're thinking this is the wrong time of year[2] to talk about healthy food,
Dr. Gourmet has a luscious menu for you. And you can tell your guests, when they're
licking their fingers, that your holiday meal was recommended by a doctor. When's
the last time you got to say that in a sentence?

The future of medicine is food
by Deena Shanker, *Quartz*

In between anatomy and biochemistry, medical students in the United States are
learning how to sauté, simmer, and season healthy, homemade meals. Since 2012,
first and second year students at Tulane University School of Medicine in Louisiana
have been learning how to cook. Since the program launched, Tulane has built the
country's first med school-affiliated teaching kitchen and become the first medical
school to count a chef as a full-time instructor.

Sixteen med schools have now licensed the center's curriculum, as have two
non-medical schools, the Children's Hospital San Antonio-Sky Lakes Residency
Program, and the Nursing School at Northwest Arkansas Community College. In fact,
about 10 percent of America's medical schools are teaching their students how to cook
with Tulane's program, Tim Harlan, who leads Tulane's Goldring Center for Culinary
Medicine, told the James Beard Foundation conference last month. It also offers
continuing medical education programs with a certification for culinary medicine, for
doctors, physician assistants, nurse practitioners, pharmacists, and registered dietitians.
The program, developed with culinary school Johnson and Wales, helps doctors give
real health advice to their patients, says Harlan, who's both a chef and a doctor. As he
says in a video, "We're not talking about nutrition, we're talking about food."

"We translate the preponderance of dietary evidence," which Harlan told *Quartz*
supports the oft-praised Mediterranean diet, "for the American kitchen." That
includes consideration of cost as well as nutritional value—diet-related illnesses like
obesity are often linked to low-income communities, including the New Orleans

---

[2]The **time of year** was November, just before Thanksgiving Day in the United States. This is a time when people prepare big meals,
go to holiday parties, and generally eat more than usual, especially desserts and other fattening food.

community that Tulane's kitchen also serves. This also works out well for training would-be doctors, says Harlan, who are usually on a stringent budget themselves.

The cooking classes are supplemented with lectures, reading, and team-based problem solving as well, and though coursework begins broadly for first- and second-year students—with an overview of the Mediterranean diet and basic knife handling skills included in the first "module"—Harlan says they are developing about 30 more modules for third- and fourth-year students. Those will focus on specific ailments like congestive heart failure, HIV, and celiac disease.

Fans of the program, including both doctors and chefs, are hoping it will be part of a major shift in the way doctors communicate with their patients about nutrition, especially amid rising rates of obesity and other diet-related illnesses. Currently fewer than half of American primary care physicians offer their patients specific guidance on diet, physical activity or weight control, a 2011 study found. "The fact that doctors are now learning to cook is like a revolution," said Sam Kass, a former White House chef and senior nutrition policy advisor, at the James Beard conference.

While it's still early days for the Tulane program, two separate studies have shown its effectiveness—for both the patients and med students alike. (Both studies included authors from the Goldring Center.) The first, which looked at patients with Type 2 Diabetes, found, for example, that those who participated in the program saw a major drop in total cholesterol, while those who did not participate saw an increase. The second found that medical students also benefited: They not only thought nutrition advice was important for their patients, but for themselves, too. By the second year, the participating med students were eating significantly more fruit and vegetables than they had previously.

Harlan expects a sea change to take place in the way doctors treat chronic illness—and the way insurance charges for it. At the conference, Kass described a future where doctors write recipes as prescriptions and insurance companies treat food as a reimbursable expense. (There is, of course, a strong economic argument in favor of a prevention-based approach to health.) Harlan predicts that care plans will eventually include menu planning, recipes and maybe even programming to get the ingredients delivered to patients. "Call me up in ten years and let's see if that's true."

Statement Evaluation

Read the passage again. Then read the following statements. Indicate whether each statement is True (T), False (F), or Not Mentioned (NM). If a statement is false, rewrite it so that it is true. Then go back to the passage and find the information that supports your answers.

1. **T** Today, some medical schools are teaching future doctors how to cook.
_____

2. **F** Most doctors are capable of providing sound nutritional advice to their patients.
_____

3. **T** Dr. Timothy Harlan is teaching future doctors how to cook.
_____

4. **F** The majority of adults living in New Orleans are in excellent physical condition.
_____

5. **F** 64 percent of the adults in New Orleans have diabetes, heart disease, or high blood pressure.
_____

6. **T** More and more medical schools are teaching cooking to their students.
_____

7. **F** A number of medical schools now have chefs as full-time instructors.
_____

8. **T** People in low-income communities seem to have diet-related illnesses.
_____

9. **F** American doctors are looking forward to learning how to communicate with their patients about nutrition.
_____

10. **F** Medical students who participated in the program did not change their eating habits.
_____

Reading Analysis

Read each question carefully. Circle the letter or number of the correct answer, or write your answer in the space provided.

1. Read lines 1–3. **Prospective** means
   a. future.
   b. practicing.
   c. traditional.

2. Read lines 6–10.
   a. A **go-to** is
      1. a path you can take.
      2. a person you can rely on.
      3. a place you can go.
   b. **Polls** are
      1. patients.
      2. statistics.
      3. surveys.
   c. According to these sentences, some doctors would not give nutrition advice
      1. because they do not have enough knowledge about it.
      2. because they do not think it is part of their job.
      3. because it goes against the Hippocratic oath.
   d. Hippocrates believed that, to be healthy,
      1. food is better than medicine.
      2. medicine is better than food.

3. Read lines 11–12. This sentence means that, to carry out Hippocrates' instruction,
   a. doctors need to learn about nutrition.
   b. doctors need to prescribe broccoli instead of drugs.
   c. doctors need to become more widely known.

4. Read lines 15–16. **Would-be** means
   a. potential.
   b. unsuccessful.
   c. eager.

5. Read lines 17–20.

    a. A **gourmet** cook is

        1. a person who talks to the media.

        2. an expert on food and cooking.

        3. a doctor who is also a chef.

    b. **Focus** means

        1. knowledge base.

        2. best idea.

        3. center of attention.

6. Read lines 22–25.

    a. The first sentence means that

        1. doctors do not speak to their patients in a practical way about how to cook healthy food.

        2. doctors do not clearly explain the basics of nutrition to their patients.

        3. doctors do not understand how to change their patients' diets.

    b. **Ingredients** means

        1. inexpensive food.

        2. good-tasting food.

        3. food items in a recipe.

    c. **Cater to** means

        1. buy food for someone.

        2. satisfy someone's needs.

        3. save money for something.

7. Read lines 26–27.

    a. **Obese** means

        1. older than most people.

        2. sicker than average.

        3. heavier than is healthy.

    b. **Overweight** means

        1. heavier than normal.

        2. more knowledgeable than most people.

        3. more worried than usual.

8. Read lines 29–30. In this context, **literature** refers to

    a. published medical research.

    b. novels and short stories.

    c. books by famous authors.

9. Read lines 33–35.
   a. A **primary care physician** is a doctor you go to
      1. if you need surgery.
      2. for a special illness.
      3. for regular medical care.
   b. **Hypertensive** medicine is used to treat
      1. high blood pressure.
      2. heart disease.
      3. diabetes.

10. Read lines 39–41.
   a. The first sentence means that
      1. it gets cold at this time of year, so it's not a good time to talk about what we eat.
      2. any time of year is not the best time to talk about eating healthy food.
      3. people often eat rich food at this time of year, so it's not a good time to talk about eating healthy food.
   b. **Luscious** means
      1. messy.
      2. delicious.
      3. wet.

11. Read lines 43–44. **Homemade meals** are
   a. made by hand from fresh ingredients.
   b. made at home from fresh or from packaged food.
   c. made from packaged or frozen food.

12. Read lines 46–48.
   a. **Launched** means
      1. grew.
      2. succeeded.
      3. began.
   b. **Affiliated** means
      1. supported.
      2. connected.
      3. produced.

13. Read lines 51–55. **Culinary** refers to

    a. health.

    b. medicine.

    (c.) cooking.

14. Read lines 60–64.

    a. **Preponderance** means

        1. the most convincing part.

        (2.) the greater part.

        3. the most understandable part.

    b. The **Mediterranean diet** refers to

        1. a diet that always has low cost and high nutritional value.

        (2.) the healthy diet of people living near the Mediterranean Sea.

        3. fresh seafood taken from the Mediterranean Sea.

    c. In the first sentence, Harlan means

        1. they turn research on health and diet into practical cooking advice for Americans.

        2. they take research on health and diet and make it easier for Americans to understand.

        3. they take evidence from research and make it a Mediterranean diet for Americans.

15. Read lines 66–68. **Supplemented** means

    (a.) enhanced.

    b. replaced.

    c. explained.

16. Read lines 70–71. **Ailments** means

    (a.) illnesses.

    b. questions.

    c. diets.

17. Read lines 72–74. **Amid** means

    a. because of.

    (b.) in the middle of.

    c. in spite of.

18. Read lines 87–90.

    a. **A sea change** means

        (1.) a transformation.

        2. a change in diet.

        3. a change in charges.

    b. **Chronic** means

        (1.) continuous.

        2. fatal.

        3. serious.

c. A **reimbursable** expense means
   1. you will pay a lot of money.
   2. you will be refunded your money.
   3. you will pay insurance for it.

19. Read lines 90–91. A **prevention-based** approach to health
    a. involves treating people when they are ill and getting them healthy as quickly as possible.
    b. involves keeping people healthy rather than treating them when they become ill.

20. What is the main idea of the passage?
    a. Many medical schools are incorporating Tulane's curriculum into their medical programs.
    b. Many medical schools are beginning to teach cooking so doctors can help people learn to prepare nutritional food and become healthier.
    c. Many people have unhealthy diets and take too much medication, so doctors are trying to change their habits.

Vocabulary Skills

PART 1

Recognizing Word Forms

In English, the verb and noun forms of some words are the same, for example, *benefit (n.)*, *benefit (v.)*.

Complete each sentence with the correct form of the word on the left. Then circle *(v.)* if you are using a verb or *(n.)* if you are using a noun. Use the correct form of the verb in either the affirmative or the negative. The nouns may be singular or plural.

focus

1. Some medical school classes for prospective doctors _____focus_____ on
   (n., v.)

   nutrition and diet. Dr. Harlan of the Goldring Center for Culinary Medicine at

   Tulane says the _____Focus_____ is on practical talk about food.
   (n., v.)

offer

2. Most American medical schools _____ offer _____ their students classes
   (n., *v.*)
   about food and diet. However, Tulane provides cooking classes to both

   students and practicing doctors. These _____ offers _____ are made to
   (*n.*, v.)
   people in the community.

cost

3. The food courses take into consideration the _____ cost _____ of the food.
   (*n.*, v.)
   Many of the people in the community, as well as the medical students, have low

   incomes, so it's important that a healthy diet _____ not cost _____ too much.
   (n., *v.*)

launch

4. The new program at Tulane University School of Medicine in

   Louisiana _____ was launched _____ in 2012. With this _____ launch _____, Tulane
   (n., *v.*)   (n., v.)
   become the first medical school to count a chef as a full-time instructor.

increase

5. Patients with Type 2 Diabetes who participated in the program at the

   Goldring Center saw a major drop in total cholesterol, while cholesterol levels

   _____ Increased _____ among those who did not participate. The researchers
   (*n.*, v.)
   believe that the _____ increase _____ in cholesterol levels was due to poor diet
   (*n.*, v.)
   and nutrition.

PART 2

Using a Dictionary

In English, words may have more than one meaning, depending on the context. For example, *develop* may mean to make into something more complete, greater, or bigger. (*They developed a program to reduce the rate of diabetes.*) It may also mean to happen, occur, transpire. (*Before making any plans, let's see what develops when the storm hits.*) In addition, *develop* can mean to change a place by building. (*They're going to develop this open land into a shopping center.*)

1. Read the following sentence. Use the context to help you understand the word in bold. Then read the dictionary entry for **count** and circle the appropriate definition.

    Tulane has built the country's first med school-affiliated teaching kitchen and become the first medical school to **count** a chef as a full-time instructor.

    ---
    count /kaunt/ *v.* [T] **1** to add up, calculate: *I counted my suits one by one.* **2** [I;T] to say numbers in order: *to count to three* **3** [T] to consider, think of: *I count her as one of my best friends.* **4** [I] to be of importance, to matter: *Having money counts because you can't do much without it.*
    ---

2. Circle the letter of the sentence that has the appropriate meaning of **count**.
    (a.) Tulane has built the country's first med school-affiliated teaching kitchen and become the first medical school to think of a chef as a full-time instructor.
    b. Tulane has built the country's first med school-affiliated teaching kitchen and become the first medical school to calculate a chef as a full-time instructor.
    c. Tulane has built the country's first med school-affiliated teaching kitchen and become the first medical school to have a chef matter as a full-time instructor.
    d. Tulane has built the country's first med school-affiliated teaching kitchen and become one of the first medical schools to number a chef in order as a full-time instructor.

3. **Count** means
    a. signify.
    (b.) consider.
    c. add up.

4. Read the following sentence. Use the context to help you understand the word in bold. Then read the dictionary entry for **serve** and circle the appropriate definition.

    That includes consideration of cost as well as nutritional value—diet-related illnesses like obesity are often linked to low-income communities, including the New Orleans community that Tulane's kitchen also **serves**.

> **serve** /sɜrv/ *v.* **served, serving, serves**   **1** [I;T] to act or function as: *This table can serve as a desk.*   **2** [I;T] to act as a servant, clerk, server, etc.: *The waitress served me coffee.*   **3** [I;T] to be in public office: *The mayor served four years.*   **4** [I;T] to put a ball into play: *to serve in tennis*

5. Circle the letter of the sentence that has the appropriate meaning of **serve**.

 a. That includes consideration of cost as well as nutritional value—diet-related illnesses like obesity are often linked to low-income communities, including the New Orleans community that Tulane's kitchen also puts into play.

 b. That includes consideration of cost as well as nutritional value—diet-related illnesses like obesity are often linked to low-income communities, including the New Orleans community that Tulane's kitchen workers are in public office for.

 c. That includes consideration of cost as well as nutritional value—diet-related illnesses like obesity are often linked to low-income communities, including the New Orleans community that Tulane's kitchen also assists.

 d. That includes consideration of cost as well as nutritional value—diet-related illnesses like obesity are often linked to low-income communities, including the New Orleans community that Tulane's kitchen also functions as.

6. **Serve** means

 a. act in a specific role.

 b. to be of assistance to.

 c. begin a ball game.

7. Read the following sentence. Use the context to help you understand the word in bold. Then read the dictionary entry for **shift** and circle the appropriate definition.

 Fans of the program, including both doctors and chefs, are hoping it will be part of a major **shift** in the way doctors communicate with their patients about nutrition.

> **shift** /ʃɪft/ *n.*   **1** a change in position or location: *a shift of money from one bank to another*   **2** a change of ideas: *a political shift from right to left*   **3** a segment of work time: *The night shift begins at 11:00 P.M.*   **4** a simple dress

8. Circle the letter of the sentence that has the appropriate meaning of **shift**.

 a. Fans of the program, including both doctors and chefs, are hoping it will be part of a major simple dress in the way doctors communicate with their patients about nutrition.

 b. Fans of the program, including both doctors and chefs, are hoping it will be part of a major segment of work time in the way doctors communicate with their patients about nutrition.

 c. Fans of the program, including both doctors and chefs, are hoping it will be part of a major change in location in the way doctors communicate with their patients about nutrition.

 d. Fans of the program, including both doctors and chefs, are hoping it will be part of a major change of ideas in the way doctors communicate with their patients about nutrition.

9. **Shift** means
   a. a specific period of working time.
   b. a move to another place.
   c. a move to a different way of thinking.

Vocabulary in Context

caters *(v.)*	launched *(v.)*	preponderance *(n.)*	reimbursable *(adj.)*
focused *(v.)*	luscious *(adj.)*	prospective *(adj.)*	supplement *(v.)*
gourmet *(adj.)*	obese *(adj.)*		

Read the following sentences. Complete each sentence with the correct word from the box. Use each word only once.

1. The deposit on plastic bottles and cans is _reimbursable_. You will get your money back when you return them.

2. My parents enjoy going to a(n) _gourmet_ restaurant every year on their wedding anniversary.

3. Many instructors _supplement_ the required textbook with articles from other sources.

4. Many people in this country are _obese_ due to poor nutrition and lack of exercise.

5. My son is a(n) _prospective_ lawyer. He is in his final year of law school.

6. Mr. Chin is a pediatric dentist. In other words, he _caters_ to young children.

7. Carla made a(n) _luscious_ pasta dish for dinner. I enjoyed it!

8. The university _launched_ a new program for retired people in the community who were interested in taking cooking classes.

9. There is a(n) _preponderance_ of information about health and nutrition online, which is easily accessible to most people.

10. Last year Kira _focused_ on learning English before she began taking college classes.

Reading Skill

Using a Graphic Organizer to Understand Problems and Solutions

Graphic organizers help you visualize information presented in a text. They can help you organize problems and connect them with their solutions.

Read the passage again. Then complete the following graphic organizer.

Writing Recipes Instead of Prescriptions: Health through Diet

Problems:
- Doctors don't trained in nutrition but it is affects pp health
- More and more people in the us are fat.

Reasons for the Problems:
- Doctors don't learn nutritions.
- People eat too much junk food.

Solutions:
- Teach doctors nutrition s
- Teach people to eat healthy.
- Give people advice.

Results:
- People eat healtier
- Doctor get more than proffesor.
- People get slim.

Information Recall

Review the information in the graphic organizer. Then answer the questions.

1. Why is there a rising rate of obesity and other diet-related illnesses?

   People does not eat healty.

2. Why does Tulane provide cooking classes to people in the community?

   Help people to eat healty.

3. Why did the health of the participants in the program improve?

   Help people eat healthy and get out of nutritional problems.

4. What was the effect of the Tulane curriculum on the medical students?

   Medical Students know nutritions.

Writing a Summary

When writing a summary, it is important to include only main ideas. Use your own words; do not copy from the reading.

Write a brief summary of the passage. It should not be more than five sentences. Use your own words. Be sure to indent the first sentence.

_____

_____

_____

_____

_____

_____

_____

Another Perspective

Read the article and answer the questions that follow.

CD 1
TR 19

Six Basic Principles of Using Food as Medicine

by Dr. James S. Gordon, *mindbodygreen.com*

In 1973, when I was a researcher at the National Institute of Mental Health and beginning to become interested in alternative therapies, I met Shyam Singha, a London-based Indian osteopath, naturopath, herbalist, acupuncturist, homeopath, and meditation master.

5   Shortly after meeting Shyam, I was crippled by a back injury. The orthopedists were issuing dire warnings and getting me ready for a surgery I didn't want. Desperate, I called Shyam in London. "Eat three pineapples a day, and nothing else for a week," he said. He explained, using principles of Chinese medicine, how the pineapple would

"work on your lung," which was the "mother of the kidney," and that the kidney was "connected" to the back. It made no sense to me then, but I knew that Shyam knew many things that I didn't. Amazingly, the pineapple worked fast.

Ever since, I too have been committed to using food as medicine. Soon I was reading scientific studies that were validating the therapeutic power of traditional remedies and suggesting the need to eliminate or cut down on foods that had become staples of the standard American diet. The basic principles are simple and straightforward:

1. Eat in harmony with your genetic programming.

Consider a whole foods plant-based diet with as little processed food and added sugar as possible. Ideally, this means consuming far fewer grains; little or no dairy; cold water fish like salmon, sardines and mackerel as the preferred animal product; and far more fiber—we consume a paltry average of 15 grams a day.

2. Use foods rather than supplements to treat and prevent chronic illness.

Whole foods contain a number of substances that work synergistically and may be far more effective than supplements that just deliver one of them. Why take the powerful antioxidant lycopene in a pill when you can eat a tomato that contains both lycopene and a number of other antioxidants, along with vitamins, minerals and other nutrients that work together to prevent heart disease by decreasing cholesterol and lipid levels and stopping abnormal blood clotting?

3. Combine your nutritional plan with a program to reduce stress and raise awareness about how, as well as what, we eat.

Stress inhibits and interferes with every aspect of digestive functioning and with the efficient use of nutrients. Learning to eat slowly and mindfully will increase your enjoyment of meals, reduce your consumption of food (most of us eat so fast we don't have time to register signals from our stomach that we are full), and help you make food choices that are better for you.

4. Understand that we are all, as the pioneering biochemist Roger Williams pointed out 50 years ago, biochemically unique.

We may be the same age and ethnicity, have very similar health status and income, but you may use 100 times as much B6 as I do, and I may require 100 times more zinc.

Sometimes we may need a nutritionally oriented physician, dietician or nutritionist to do specific, sophisticated tests to determine our deficiencies and requirements. We can always learn a great deal about what's good for us by experimenting with different diets and foods, and by paying close attention to the outcomes.

5. Find a health professional who will help you begin treatment of chronic conditions with nutrition and stress management (as well as exercise) rather than medication.

Except in life-threatening situations, this is the sane, common sense way to go. The prescription antacids, Type 2 diabetes drugs, and antidepressants that tens of millions of Americans use to decrease acid reflux, lower blood sugar, and improve mood, only treat symptoms and do not address causes. And they have very significant and often dangerous side-effects.

6. Don't become a food fanatic.

Use these guidelines (and others that make sense to you), but don't beat yourself up for deviating from them. Just notice the effect of a questionable choice, learn, and return to your program.

Questions for Another Perspective

1. What experience made Dr. Gordon decide to commit to using food as medicine?

   _____

   _____

2. Why is a whole foods diet superior to taking supplements such as lycopene?

   _____

   _____

3. How does eating slowly and mindfully help improve our health?

   _____

   _____

4. Why is our choice of physician so important in maintaining our health through diet?

   _____

   _____

5. What is one problem with many medications?

   _____

   _____

Topics for Discussion and Writing

1. Why is a low income so often associated with a poor diet and bad health?

2. Do you eat mostly homemade food, or do you often go out to eat? Which do you think is better for your health? Why? Discuss this with a partner and compare your answers.

3. There is an ancient saying, "When diet is wrong, medicine is of no use. When diet is correct, medicine is of no need." What does this proverb mean?

4. Do you think food can replace medicine for some illnesses? Why or why not? Give examples and explain your answer.

5. Write in your journal. There is a saying, "You are what you eat." What does this saying mean to you? Do you agree with it? Explain the reasons for your answer.

Critical Thinking

1. Many people would prefer to take a pill for a medical problem simply because it is easier than making a major change in their lifestyle. How might a doctor help these people be motivated to change the way they plan meals, shop for food, and cook?

2. Companies that manufacture drugs make billions of dollars a year. How might they react to doctors reducing prescriptions in favor of teaching people how to cook healthier meals?

3. Why do you think the health of the medical students in Tulane's program improved? Explain your reasons.

4. According to the second article, only about 10 percent of America's medical schools are teaching their students how to cook with Tulane's program. Why do you think this number is so low? Do you think more medical schools will adopt this type of program in the future? Explain your answers.

5. In the first readings, what are Christina Farr's and Deena Shanker's viewpoints on food as medicine? How are their approaches to the concept similar? How are they different?

Crossword Puzzle

Review the words in the box below. Then read the clues on the next page. Write the words in the correct spaces in the puzzle.

affiliated	fatal	hypertensive	obese	prevention
ailments	focus	ingredients	overweight	prospective
caters	gourmet	launch	polls	reimbursable
chronic	homemade	luscious	preponderance	supplement
culinary				

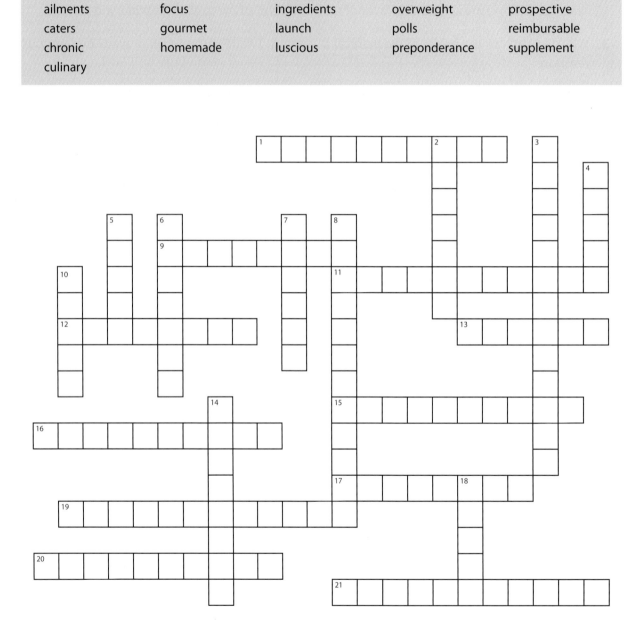

Crossword Puzzle Clues

ACROSS CLUES

1. Being _____ isn't necessarily unhealthy, but continued weight gain may be a problem.

9. My mother never buys cakes from a store. All her cakes are _____.

11. I don't have all the _____ for this meal. I need to go to the supermarket to buy them.

12. Kim's son wants to go to a(n) _____ school to learn cooking and restaurant management.

13. Michael's organization _____ to people in need by supplying them with healthy food.

15. Even if your diet is nutritious, you may need to _____ it with extra vitamins.

16. Teaching people to cook healthy meals is part of the concept of _____ rather than treatment.

17. Sam loves to bake. He creates many _____ desserts when he has company for dinner.

19. If you have high blood pressure, you must take medicine to treat your _____ condition.

20. My primary care physician is _____ with the best hospital in the city.

21. _____ doctors and even chefs-in-training need to learn the nutritional value of all kinds of food.

DOWN CLUES

2. My sister is a(n) _____ chef. She graduated from a well-known cooking school, first in her class.

3. The _____ of research supports a healthy diet to maintain health.

4. Future _____ of doctors will hopefully indicate more physicians who teach patients to cook healthy meals.

5. It's possible that some _____ diseases could be avoided through proper diet and exercise.

6. Not all _____ diseases are permanent. Some can be cured.

7. Lee plans to _____ a small business that brings nutritious fruit and vegetables to low-income areas.

8. The cost of food is not a(n) _____ expense. Insurance companies will not give you any money back.

10. A diet should _____ first on nutrition, and second on losing weight.

14. Xiao Lin suffers from several _____ and needs to see a doctor once a month.

18. _____ people may develop serious illnesses. It's important for them to lose weight.

Our World and Beyond

1. What challenges do we face today in trying to preserve Earth's natural resources?

2. Is it possible to save species that are in danger of disappearing? Can species that have died out come back to life?

3. Is there life on other planets? If so, what might it be like?

211

CHAPTER 10 What is sustainable living?

Prereading

1. Look at the title and the photos above. What do you think sustainable living means?

2. Sustainable living means to have a lifestyle that includes (check (✓) all that apply):

   _____ eating a lot of fresh vegetables

   _____ buying and using only what you need

   _____ wasting natural resources

   _____ recycling paper and plastics

   _____ saving energy (for example, gas and electricity)

3. Do you think sustainable living is important? Why or why not?

Reading

🎧 **Read the passage carefully. Then complete the exercises that follow.**

CD 1
TR 20

What is sustainable living?

Conserve Energy Future

Sustainable living is the practice of reducing your demand on natural resources by making sure that you replace what you use to the best of your ability. Sometimes that can mean not choosing to consume a product that is made using practices that don't promote sustainability, and sometimes it means changing how you do things so that
5   you start becoming more of an active part of the cycle of life.

We all know that climate change, global warming, depletion of the ozone (O_3) layer,[1] and resource depletion are real and their impact on human and animal lives can be devastating. It is an opportunity for people to adopt actions for sustainable living that can help them to reduce their carbon (C) footprint or environmental impact
10   by altering their lifestyle. Simple measures like using public transportation more often, reducing energy consumption, becoming more eco-friendly can go a long way in reducing your environmental impact and making this planet a clean and safe place.

Fifteen Easy Ways to Practice Sustainable Living

Want to start practicing sustainable living? It is easier than you think. Here are 15 easy suggestions to get you started.

1. Become a Member of a Community Garden

15   It isn't just about growing your own food. Being a member of a community garden helps to promote sustainable living in your area. Gardens create green spaces and the garden waste such as dead flowers can be mulched and returned to support healthy soil. Green spaces aren't just important for your state of mind; in urban areas they can play an important role in offsetting carbon (C) emissions.

2. Practice Minimalism

20   Minimalism doesn't mean living without anything; it means that you are making sure that everything you own and use is put to its maximum purpose. This means waste materials as well. With a minimalist lifestyle, you will recycle more, and be more mindful of the items you support being produced so that sustainability is emphasized.

---

[1] The **ozone (O_3) layer** is a part of the upper atmosphere that helps block dangerous radiation from the sun and keep it from reaching the surface of Earth.

3. Change the Lights in Your House

By changing the lighting in your home from traditional light bulbs to CFLs (compact fluorescent light bulbs) and using skylights and more natural light, you will reduce your demand on energy resources significantly. Using longer lasting, energy efficient light sources also reduces the amount of waste going into landfills.

4. Become More Efficient with Your Errands

You don't have to buy a hybrid to reduce your reliance on fossil fuels. By choosing to become more efficient with your errands, you can create a system of sustainable living that is based on reducing the amount of natural resources you consume.

5. Start Using Natural Cleaners

Take an hour or so to research some homemade options for natural cleaners. Vinegar and water can clean most surfaces, and the saponin[2] from quinoa is a natural laundry detergent. By using natural cleaners, you are reducing the amount of plastic packaging being made and the amount of chemicals that are being introduced to the water system.

6. Walk, Bike, or Car Pool to Work

The less personal use of your car you make, the more you and the environment will benefit. Sustainable living not only promotes sustainability by reducing pollution and the consumption of natural resources; walking or biking to work will also improve your health and reduce the demand on public health resources. Even car pooling assists sustainability as it can provide an increased social outlet that can improve the quality of life. Science has found that there is a direct connection between your quality of life and the sustainability of life that you choose to lead.

7. Spend More Time Reading and Playing Games

How can this be a part of sustainable living? By reducing your reliance on entertainment forms that require energy and natural resources, you can help to reduce the demand and drain on them.

8. Try to Get on a More Natural Sleep Schedule

Getting on a natural sleep schedule means becoming more attuned to the natural light in the day. Not only is this better for your health, it will begin to lessen the amount of power that you use while you are up.

9. Reduce, Reuse, and Recycle

Reduce your need to buy new products. If there is less waste, then there is less to recycle or reuse. Learning to reuse items, or repurpose them for different uses than what they are intended for, is essential in waste hierarchy. Recycle old glass bottles or aluminum cans. Keep a recycle bin at your home and try making more trips to recycling stations than to the landfill.

---

[2] **Saponin** is a naturally occurring chemical compound that is found in more than 100 species of plants.

10. Unplug Devices When Not in Use

55   Most electronic devices keep on drawing electricity even when they're off. To reduce energy usage, simply pull the plug when not in use. It will help you to save energy and reduce your monthly electricity bill.

11. Buy the Right-Sized House

Practitioners of sustainable living conduct their lives in ways that are consistent with sustainability. Among the many ways that promote sustainability, one of them is
60   buying a smaller house that is going to consume less energy compared to a big house. You're going to spend less on lighting, furniture, and overall furnishing. You can even purchase items from thrift stores and donate them again when they're no longer needed. Make use of green home building ideas and techniques while building a new home.

12. Use Daylight as Much as Possible

65   Sunlight is free and doesn't cost anything. Using sunlight during the day helps to reduce dependence on fossil fuels to produce electricity and your bulbs and tube lights are going to last longer.

13. Stop Unwanted Mail

Save natural resources by opting out of billions of unwanted mailings and simplify your life. Many websites offer free services to opt out of catalogs, coupons, credit
70   card offers, phone books, circulars, and more. It helps you to reduce clutter, protect privacy, and save the environment.

14. Practice Keeping a "Zero Energy Balance" Budget

A zero energy balance budget means that what you take in, you also return back. This is really the core of all sustainable living. If you practice keeping a budget that has a zero energy balance, you will be surprised how your habits of consuming will
75   change and reduce your imprint on the world.

15. Change Your Washing Habits

This last one is important to attain sustainable living. We wash everything too much. Not only has science discovered that our over emphasis on being clean has reduced our natural immune resistance to diseases (which require exposure to bacteria to develop), but each person wastes tremendous amounts of water when
80   they bathe, wash dishes, or do laundry. Practice taking short, timed showers, washing dishes in a sink of water and then rinsing them, and cutting down on the amount of laundry that you do.

Volunteers work on a community garden

Statement Evaluation

Read the passage again. Then read the following statements. Indicate whether each statement is True (T), False (F), or an Inference (I). If a statement is false, rewrite it so that it is true. Then go back to the passage and find the information that supports your answers.

1. _____ Sustainable living may involve not buying products that harmed the environment when they were manufactured.

_____

2. _____ Global warming may result in melting ice all over the world.

_____

3. _____ Garden waste is useless and should be thrown away.

_____

4. _____ Using longer lasting, energy-efficient light sources means throwing away fewer burned-out light bulbs.

_____

5. _____ Vinegar cannot be used for cleaning purposes.

_____

6. _____ Spending more time reading and playing games lessens your use of electricity.

_____

7. _____ If you turn off your electronic devices, they will stop using electricity.

_____

Reading Analysis

Read each question carefully. Circle the letter or number of the correct answer, or write your answer in the space provided.

1. Read lines 1–4.
   a. **Sustainable living** involves
      1. lowering your demand on natural resources by buying less of everything.
      2. lessening your demand on natural resources by trying your best to replace what you use.
      3. reducing your demand on natural resources by buying synthetic products.
   b. **Demand** means
      1. argument.
      2. requirement.
      3. order.
   c. **Consume** means
      1. eat.
      2. use up.
      3. purchase.
   d. **Promote** means
      1. advertise.
      2. change.
      3. support.

2. Read lines 6–10.
   a. **Depletion** means
      1. spoiling.
      2. reduction.
      3. disappearance.
   b. What is the **ozone (O_3) layer**?

_____

c. Where did you find this information?

_____

d. This type of information is called a(n)

_____

e. **Impact** means
   1. usefulness.
   2. harm.
   3. effect.

f. **Devastating** means
   1. very real.
   2. disastrous.
   3. sustainable.

g. Climate change, global warming, depletion of the ozone layer, and resource depletion
   1. can greatly harm life on Earth.
   2. may somewhat harm life on Earth.
   3. may have little effect on life on Earth.

h. **Altering** means
   1. reducing.
   2. improving.
   3. changing.

3. Read lines 10–12.

a. **Measures** means
   1. impacts.
   2. amounts.
   3. actions.

b. Using public transportation more often and reducing energy consumption
   1. will help everyone go a long way.
   2. will save everyone money.
   3. will help improve the environment.

4. Read lines 16–19.

a. **Garden waste such as dead flowers can be mulched and returned to support healthy soil.** This sentence means
   1. material such as dead plants can be burned and thrown into the trash.
   2. material such as cut grass and leaves can be spread on the ground to improve the soil.
   3. material such as rotten fruit and vegetables can be collected and thrown out.

b. **Offsetting** means
   1. getting rid of something harmful.
   2. moving something somewhere else.
   3. compensating for something negative.

5. Read lines 22–24. A **minimalist lifestyle**

   a tends to be simple and thoughtful.

   b. involves not having what you want.

   c. means not owning anything unless you can pay for it.

6. Read lines 29–31.

   a. **Reliance** means

      1. purchase.

      2. dependence.

      3. use.

   b. **You don't have to buy a hybrid to reduce your reliance on fossil fuels.** This sentence means

      1. you do not need to buy a very small car with a small engine.

      2. you do not need to buy a car that runs on batteries as well as gasoline.

7. Read lines 40–42.

   a. **Car pooling** means

      1. having one or more passengers in your car when you go to work.

      2. lending your car to other people and walking or bicycling instead.

      3. socializing with your friends when you drive your car.

   b. One of the advantages of car pooling is that

      1. you use your car less often for personal reasons.

      2. you can socialize by not being alone when you drive to work.

      3. you drive more safely because other people are in your car.

8. Read lines 47–48. **Attuned to** means

   a. responsive to.

   b. happy about.

   c. interested in.

9. Read lines 51–52.

   a. **Repurpose** means

      1. find a new use for something instead of throwing it out.

      2. use something again so you do not have to buy a new one.

      3. use something for longer than you intended to.

   b. An example of repurposing is

      1. giving away old magazines for others to read.

      2. cutting up unwanted curtains and making pillows with the material.

      3. giving away clothes you do not want to those who need them.

10. Read lines 55–56.

   a. **Unplug** means

     1. turn down.

     2. disconnect.

     3. turn off.

   b. **Drawing electricity** means

     1. using electricity.

     2. creating electricity.

     3. having electricity.

11. Read lines 61–63.

   a. A **thrift store**

     1. sells cheap products.

     2. sells used products.

     3. sells new products.

   b. **Donate** means

     1. buy at a discount.

     2. sell back cheaply.

     3. give to help others.

12. Read lines 68–71.

   a. **Opting out** means

     1. choosing not to do something.

     2. refusing to take something.

     3. returning mail to the sender.

   b. **Clutter** is

     1. a large amount of paper, books, and magazines.

     2. a large collection of disorganized items.

     3. unnecessary expense from buying items.

13. Read lines 72–73.

   a. An energy **budget** is

     1. a list of kinds of energy.

     2. a plan of expenses.

     3. an account of your electricity use.

    b. A **"zero energy balance" budget** means
       1. you use energy until there is nothing left.
       2. what you use equals what you give back.
       3. you use only what you can afford.

    c. **Core** means
       1. practice.
       2. beginning.
       3. center.

14. In line 75, **imprint** means
    a. image.
    b. effect.
    c. harm.

15. Read lines 77–82.
    a. **Resistance** means
       1. protection from.
       2. dislike of.
       3. openness about.

    b. **Wastes** means
       1. uses correctly.
       2. draws on.
       3. uses unnecessarily.

    c. When you take a **timed shower**,
       1. you record how much time your shower takes.
       2. you take a shower at a specific time.
       3. you limit the time you are in the shower.

16. What is the main idea of the passage?
    a. Sustainable living is an important practice in the 21st century.
    b. Everyone needs to practice sustainable living to save resources.
    c. Sustainable living is essential, and there are many ways to practice it.

Vocabulary Skills

> ### Recognizing Word Forms
> In English, there are several ways that verbs change to nouns. Some verbs become nouns by adding the suffix *-ion* or *-tion,* for example, *participate (v.), participation (n.).* There may be spelling changes as well.

Complete each sentence with the correct word form on the left. Use the correct form of the verb in either the affirmative or negative. The nouns may be singular or plural.

promote *(v.)*   **1.** There are many simple changes you can make in your life to aid in the

promotion *(n.)*   _____ of a sustainable lifestyle. This can sometimes mean

choosing not to use a product that _____ sustainability.

adopt *(v.)*   **2.** We can prevent continued resource depletion when we

adoption *(n.)*   _____ some actions that conserve resources. The

_____ of these simple measures can reduce our impact on

the environment.

devastate *(v.)*   **3.** Global warming, climate change, and depletion of the ozone layer

devastation *(n.)*   may cause _____ to our environment and may also

_____ human and animal life.

alter *(v.)*   **4.** By making some _____ to our lifestyles, we can reduce our

alteration *(n.)*   carbon impact on Earth. If we _____ our ways of living now,

the result will be a negative effect on the environment of the future.

consume *(v.)*   **5.** A small house _____ as much energy as a large house. The

consumption *(n.)*   reduction in energy _____ can make our planet a clean and

safe place to live.

PART 2

First, match each word or phrase with the correct meaning. Then complete each sentence with the correct word or phrase. Use each word or phrase only once.

_____ 1.	carbon (C) emissions	a.	the amount of carbon (C) released into the atmosphere as the result of a particular activity, such as driving a car
_____ 2.	carbon footprint	b.	anything that is helpful for a clean environment
_____ 3.	eco-friendly	c.	the carbon dioxide (CO_2) or carbon monoxide (CO) that is released into the air by vehicles or industrial activity
_____ 4.	fossil fuels	d.	coal, oil, and natural gas
_____ 5.	global warming	e.	the contamination of air, water, or land
_____ 6.	green spaces	f.	the increase of Earth's temperature over time
_____ 7.	natural resources	g.	materials found in nature, such as water, trees and plants, or minerals
_____ 8.	pollution	h.	open or protected areas such as parks or wilderness areas
_____ 9.	recycling	i.	the practice of reducing your demand on natural resources by replacing what you use
_____ 10.	sustainable living	j.	the practice of reusing or reprocessing materials, for example, glass or paper

1. Many industries are trying to reduce the amount of _____ created in their manufacturing processes.

2. We have begun practicing _____ in our neighborhood by setting up centers where people can go to exchange items they no longer need for something they may want.

3. Our college campus has several _____ where students can sit and study in a natural environment.

4. I am reducing my _____ by riding my bicycle to work instead of driving my car.

5. Earth's _____ are not unlimited. We need to protect them.

6. Most cities have _____ centers where plastic, glass, and metals are collected for reuse.

7. The government has established strict rules to control and reduce the _____ from motorized vehicles, such as cars, trucks, and motorcycles.

8. Oil, coal, and gas are all _____. They will run out one day, but we have an unlimited supply of solar power.

9. _____ is a proven fact. The evidence includes the melting of ice in Antarctica, Greenland, and other areas of the world.

10. We only buy household products that are _____, such as products in biodegradable containers.

Recycling center in South Island, New Zealand

Vocabulary in Context

Read the following sentences. Complete each sentence with the correct word from the box. Use each word only once.

altered *(v.)*	core *(n.)*	opt out *(v.)*	repurpose *(v.)*
attune *(v.)*	depleted *(v.)*	promote *(v.)*	resistance *(n.)*
clutter *(n.)*	measures *(n.)*		

1. I never throw away my old T-shirts. I _____ them to use as dust rags when I clean my house.

2. Carlos decided to _____ of his medical insurance plan when he found a cheaper one online.

3. Because of my grandfather's _____ to learning a new language, he refused to move to a different country with his family.

4. Many educators _____ the importance of children eating a healthy breakfast before school.

5. Soy Lin _____ her vacation plans when a hurricane struck the town she was going to visit.

6. The belief that all people are created equal is at the _____ of the American Constitution.

7. After spending years studying in the university, it was difficult for Federica to

   _____ herself to the business world.

8. Lee quickly _____ his bank account after buying textbooks for all of his courses.

9. My apartment is filled with _____ because my roommate refuses to discard old newspapers and magazines.

10. Some small _____, for example, taking the stairs instead of riding the elevator or walking to school instead of taking the bus, can help us to stay in shape.

Reading Skill

Understanding Bar Graphs and Pie Charts

Graphs and charts often contain important information. It's important to understand them. Bar graphs and pie charts often compare numbers or amounts. Both give you information about a reading.

Read the following bar graph and pie chart. Then answer the questions.

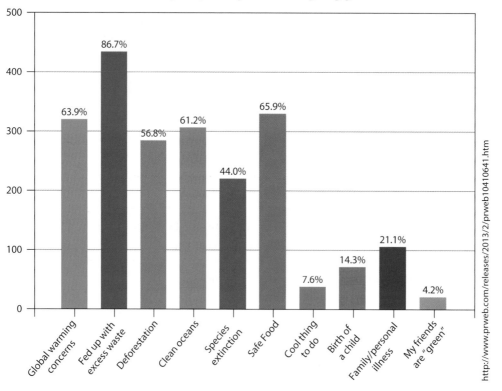

What is your primary reason for going green?

1. Recently, 560 people were surveyed regarding their main reasons for "going green." Going green means adopting a sustainable lifestyle.

   a. What is the most popular reason for going green?

   _____

   b. What is the least popular reason for going green?

   _____

c. Based on this survey, what can you conclude about the reasons most people go green?
   1. They are influenced by their friends and family.
   2. They are concerned about the environment.
   3. They want a healthier lifestyle.

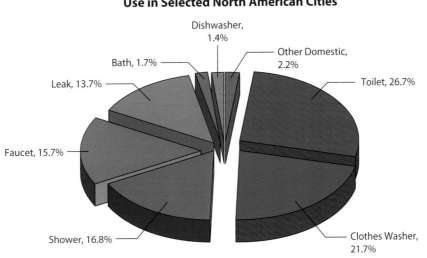

Survey of Indoor Per Capita Water Use in Selected North American Cities

Dishwasher, 1.4%
Other Domestic, 2.2%
Bath, 1.7%
Leak, 13.7%
Toilet, 26.7%
Faucet, 15.7%
Clothes Washer, 21.7%
Shower, 16.8%

2. a. According to the pie chart, what accounts for the highest amount of water used?

_____

b. What accounts for the second highest amount of water used?

_____

c. Which accounts for more water use: showers or baths?

_____

d. Which item in the pie chart is the most wasteful use of water?

_____

Information Recall

Review the information in the bar graph and pie chart. Then answer the questions.

1. Review the bar graph. What do the first five reasons for going green have in common?

_____

_____

2. What do the other five reasons for going green have in common?

_____

_____

3. Based on the information in the pie chart, what three recommendations could you make for reducing water consumption in the home?

a. _____

b. _____

c. _____

Writing a Summary

When writing a summary, it is important to include only main ideas. Use your own words; do not copy from the reading.

Write a brief summary of the passage. It should not be more than five sentences. Use your own words. Be sure to indent the first sentence.

_____

_____

_____

_____

_____

_____

Another Perspective

🎧 **Read the article and answer the questions that follow.**

A Model of Efficiency: NASA's Sustainability Base

National Aeronautics and Space Administration

In 2007, NASA held a 'Renovation by Replacement' (RbR) competition. RbR is designed to replace antiquated and inefficient buildings with new, energy-efficient buildings. Each of the agency's ten centers submitted proposals to build a new facility, and Ames Research Center won the contest.

5 Steve Zornetzer, Associate Center Director for NASA Ames saw an opportunity to take the closed-loop thinking[1] that NASA uses in space exploration and apply it to a green building on Earth.

Although most people associate NASA with space, NASA is also committed to advancing technology and innovations that will help solve the critical challenges that

10 are facing Earth. As NASA Ames Center Director Pete Worden says, "This tiny planet we share is our only home."

NASA has decades of experience in creating human environments that promote optimal functioning. In order for astronauts to do their jobs, they have to be at peak function, mentally and physically. Everything in their environment is designed to

15 support that. Similarly, Sustainability Base was created with the vision that everything about the design would support both human and planetary well-being.

Through a combination of NASA innovations, as well as commercially available technologies, Sustainability Base leaves virtually no footprint. The project is proof not only that this level of sustainable building is possible, but also that it is imperative for

20 the health of our planet.

Workplace Innovations

From the moment they arrive, each of the 210 people who work at Sustainability Base experience openness and abundant connections to nature. The lobby is open through both floors and suffused with daylight. A large LCD display shows visitors and employees how much energy the building is using and where that energy

25 comes from.

The building is narrow, which means that everyone benefits from the daylight that pours in through the floor-to-ceiling windows and skylights. The large windows also provide a constant flow of fresh air, and people can establish a visual and emotional connection to the surrounding landscape.

---

[1] **Closed-loop thinking** in spacecraft involves recycling and reusing resources on board the spacecraft. For example, all available air and water are recycled and reused within the spacecraft itself.

30   Outside, people can have meetings in various naturally landscaped "rooms" amidst gardens and trees, or they can sit on benches or at picnic tables and simply work quietly in harmony with nature. Those who work at Sustainability Base are an integral part of keeping the building sustainable. Each individual has a personal energy dashboard that shows their energy usage at any given moment and even suggests
35 energy conservation activities, as simple as lowering the shades or opening windows.

Sustainability in Action

    Sustainability Base is one of the greenest Federal buildings ever constructed. It is designed to go beyond 'not hurting' the environment to actually being beneficial to nature and humans. Sustainability Base generates all the power it needs to operate and uses 90 percent less drinking water than a traditional building of comparable
40 size.

    The building also generates a considerable amount of its own renewable power through a variety of solar panels, a highly efficient fuel cell and a small wind turbine. The materials used to build and furnish Sustainability Base were locally procured and, in many cases, include recycled elements—for example, the oak planks that line
45 the second-floor lobby were reclaimed from an old NASA wind tunnel.

NASA Sustainability Base

Questions for Another Perspective

1. What are some ways that NASA has applied the closed-loop concept to its Sustainability Base?

   _____

   _____

   _____

2. How does the design of Sustainability Base support the well-being of the people who work there?

   _____

   _____

   _____

3. What are some ways that Sustainability Base saves energy?

   _____

   _____

   _____

4. What are some ways that the design of Sustainability Base helps the environment?

   _____

   _____

   _____

Topics for Discussion and Writing

1. Work with two or three classmates. Review the list of 15 ways we can practice sustainable living. As a group, put the 15 ways into what you consider their order of importance. As a class, decide on the ten most important ways.

15 Ways to Practice Sustainable Living	Your Group's Order of Importance
Become a member of a community garden.	1. _____
Practice minimalism.	2. _____
Change the lights in your house.	3. _____
Become more efficient with your errands.	4. _____
Start using natural cleaners.	5. _____
Walk, bike, or car pool to work.	6. _____
Spend more time reading and playing games.	7. _____
Try to get on a more natural sleep schedule.	8. _____
Reduce, reuse, and recycle.	9. _____
Unplug devices when not in use.	10. _____
Buy the right-sized house.	11. _____
Use daylight as much as possible.	12. _____
Stop unwanted mail.	13. _____
Practice keeping a "zero energy balance" budget.	14. _____
Change your washing habits.	15. _____

2. Work in small groups. Each group will select two or three of the ways to practice sustainable living so that each group has different ways, and all 15 ways are chosen. In your group, add to the details given in the reading for each of the ways you have selected. See the example that follows.

Ways Your Group Has Chosen	Additional Details for Each Way
Walk, bike, or car pool to work.	In addition to walking, biking, or car pooling to work or school, take a bus or a train.

3. What are some examples of items in your home that you no longer want, but that you can repurpose for a different use than what they were originally intended for?

4. Write in your journal. What are some ways you can incorporate sustainable living into your daily life?

Critical Thinking

1. What are some of the benefits of sustainable living to individuals? What are some benefits of sustainable living to communities? Give examples for each and explain your answer.

2. Do you think the ideas in NASA's Sustainability Base could be applied to other buildings? Why or why not?

3. Why do you think sustainable living is important to Earth? What could be the consequences if we don't adopt a sustainable lifestyle?

4. The article in Another Perspective describes NASA's Sustainability Base. How many of the suggestions in the first reading have been implemented in the base? What other suggestions could the Sustainability Base implement?

5. What is the author's purpose in publishing "What is Sustainable Living?" in *Conserve Energy Future?*

Crossword Puzzle

Review the words in the box below. Then read the clues on the next page. Write the words in the correct spaces in the puzzle.

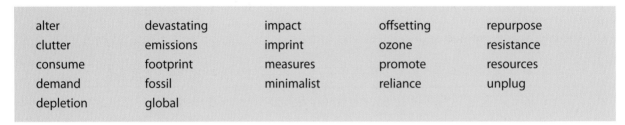

alter	devastating	impact	offsetting	repurpose
clutter	emissions	imprint	ozone	resistance
consume	footprint	measures	promote	resources
demand	fossil	minimalist	reliance	unplug
depletion	global			

Crossword Puzzle Clues

ACROSS CLUES

1. _____ fuels are composed of plants that died many millions of years ago.

6. The students competed to develop the best ideas to _____ items that are no longer needed.

7. Electric cars and hybrid cars help reduce our _____ on gasoline and diesel fuel.

8. Our "carbon _____" refers to our negative effect on the environment.

12. We can _____ sound habits by showing our children how to reuse and recycle.

14. Every evening I _____ the electronic devices in my home that I don't use at night.

17. When we conserve resources, we reduce our _____ on the environment.

18. My home is full of old newspapers and magazines. I need to get rid of the _____.

19. The _____ of useful land for agriculture could result in a disaster for humans.

21. We should not buy more than we can _____.

22. The warming of the environment will surely have _____ consequences for all.

DOWN CLUES

2. We need to think about the _____ our actions have on the environment.

3. _____ warming will result in a rise in ocean levels all over the world.

4. We must protect our natural _____, including plants, animals, air, and water.

5. Humans are losing their _____ to some diseases by trying too hard to be very clean.

9. By planting new trees to replace ones that are cut down, we are _____ the damage to the land.

10. Everything we do leaves a(n) _____ on the world we live in.

11. The _____ layer protects us from dangerous radiation from the sun.

13. Being a(n) _____ doesn't mean giving up our quality of life. In fact, it can improve it!

15. Carbon monoxide is one of the dangerous _____ that come from cars and trucks.

16. Fortunately, there are many simple _____ we can take to become eco-friendly.

20. We need to _____ our buying practices and buy only what we need.

Pyrenean ibex, a species of wild goat

Western black rhinoceros

Prereading

1. Look at the photos. What do these animals have in common?

2. What might be some of the causes of an animal's extinction?

3. Read the title of this article. How might an extinct animal be brought back to life?

🎧 **Read the passage carefully. Then complete the exercises that follow.**

CD 1
TR 22

Bringing Extinct Species Back to Life:
Is it a good idea?

by Carl Zimmer, *National Geographic*

On July 30, 2003, a team of Spanish and French scientists brought an animal back from extinction, if only to watch it become extinct again. The animal was a kind of wild goat known as a *bucardo,* or Pyrenean ibex. For thousands of years it lived high in the Pyrenees, the mountain range that divides France from Spain. Then hunters
5 drove down the bucardo population over several centuries. In 1989, Spanish scientists concluded that there were only a dozen or so left. Ten years later a single bucardo remained: a female nicknamed Celia. A team from the Ordesa and Monte Perdido National Park, led by wildlife veterinarian Alberto Fernández-Arias, caught the animal in a trap, clipped a radio collar around her neck, and released her back into the wild.
10 Nine months later the radio collar let out a signal that Celia had died. They found her crushed beneath a fallen tree. With her death, the bucardo became officially extinct.

But Celia's cells lived on, preserved in labs in Zaragoza and Madrid. Over the next few years a team of reproductive physiologists led by José Folch injected nuclei[1] from those cells into goat eggs emptied of their own DNA, then implanted the eggs
15 in surrogate mothers. After 57 implantations, one carried a clone of Celia to term. Despite the efforts to help her breathe, after a mere ten minutes Celia's clone died.

The bucardo is only one in the long list of animals humans have driven extinct. And with many more species now endangered, the bucardo will have much more company in the years to come. Fernández-Arias belongs to a small but passionate
20 group of researchers who believe that cloning can help reverse that trend.

The notion of bringing vanished species back to life—some call it de-extinction—has hovered at the boundary between reality and science fiction for more than two decades. Celia's clone is the closest that anyone has gotten to true de-extinction. Fernández-Arias, now the head of the government of Aragon's Hunting, Fishing and Wetlands department,
25 has been waiting for the moment when science would finally catch up, and humans might gain the ability to bring back an animal they had driven extinct. "We are at that moment," he told me.

I met Fernández-Arias last autumn at a closed-session scientific meeting at the National Geographic Society's headquarters in Washington, D.C. For the first time in
30 history a group of geneticists, wildlife biologists, conservationists, and ethicists had

---

[1] The **nuclei** (singular: nucleus) are the central parts of most cells. The nuclei contain genetic material (DNA).

gathered to discuss the possibility of de-extinction. Could it be done? Should it be done? A consensus was emerging: De-extinction is now within reach.

"It's gone very much further, very much more rapidly than anyone ever would've imagined," says Ross MacPhee, a curator of mammalogy at the American Museum of Natural History in New York. "What we really need to think about is why we would want to do this in the first place, to actually bring back a species."

"If we're talking about species we drove extinct, then I think we have an obligation to try to do this," says Michael Archer, a paleontologist at the University of New South Wales who has championed de-extinction for years.

Other scientists who favor de-extinction argue that there will be concrete benefits. Biological diversity is a storehouse of natural invention. Most pharmaceutical drugs, for example, were derived from natural compounds found in wild plant species, which are also vulnerable to extinction.

When Fernández-Arias first tried to bring back the bucardo ten years ago, the tools at his disposal were, in hindsight, woefully crude. Over the past decade scientists have improved their success with cloning animals. Scientists and explorers have been talking for decades about bringing back the mammoth. Their first—and so far only—achievement was to find well-preserved mammoths in the Siberian tundra. Now, armed with the new cloning technologies, researchers at the Sooam Biotech Research Foundation in Seoul have teamed up with mammoth experts from North-Eastern Federal University in the Siberian city of Yakutsk. Last summer they traveled up the Yana River, drilling tunnels into the frozen cliffs along the river. They found chunks of mammoth tissue, including bone marrow, hair, skin, and fat. The tissue is now in Seoul, where the Sooam scientists are examining it.

"If we dream about it, the ideal case would be finding a viable cell, a cell that's alive," says Sooam's Insung Hwang, who organized the Yana River expedition. If the Sooam researchers do find such a cell, they could coax it to produce millions of cells. These could be reprogrammed to grow into embryos, which could then be implanted in surrogate elephants, the mammoth's closest living relatives.

Most scientists doubt that any living cell could have survived freezing on the open tundra. But Hwang and his colleagues have a Plan B: capture an intact nucleus of a mammoth cell, which is far more likely to have been preserved than the cell itself. Cloning a mammoth from nothing but an intact nucleus, however, will be a lot trickier. The Sooam researchers will need to transfer the nucleus into an elephant egg that has had its own nucleus removed. This will require harvesting eggs from an elephant—a feat no one has yet accomplished. If the DNA inside the nucleus is well preserved enough to take control of the egg, it just might start dividing into a mammoth embryo. If the scientists can get past that hurdle, they still have the formidable task of transplanting the embryo into an elephant's womb. Then, as Zimov cautions, they will need patience. If all goes well, it will still be almost two years before they can see if the elephant will give birth to a healthy mammoth.

Even if the Sooam team fails to find an intact mammoth nucleus, someone might still bring the species back. Scientists already have the technology for reconstructing most of the genes it takes to make a mammoth, which could be inserted into an elephant stem cell.

Though the revival of a mammoth is no longer mere fantasy, the reality is still years away. "There is clearly a terrible urgency to saving threatened species and habitats," says John Wiens, an evolutionary biologist at Stony Brook University in New York. "As far as I can see, there is little urgency for bringing back extinct ones. Why invest millions of dollars in bringing a handful of species back from the dead, when there are millions still waiting to be discovered, described, and protected?"

De-extinction advocates counter that the cloning and genomic engineering technologies being developed for de-extinction could also help preserve endangered species, especially ones that don't breed easily in captivity. And though cutting-edge biotechnology can be expensive when it's first developed, it has a way of becoming very cheap very fast.

Hunting is not the only threat that would face recovered species. For many, there's no place left to call home. The Chinese river dolphin became extinct due to pollution and other pressures from the human population on the Yangtze River. Things are just as bad there today.

"Without an environment to put re-created species back into, the whole exercise is futile and a gross waste of money," says Glenn Albrecht, director of the Institute for Social Sustainability at Murdoch University in Australia.

Even if de-extinction proved a complete logistical success, the questions would not end. De-extinction advocates are pondering these questions, and most believe they need to be resolved before any major project moves forward. Hank Greely, a leading bioethicist at Stanford University, has taken a keen interest in investigating the ethical and legal implications of de-extinction. And yet for Greely, as for many others, the very fact that science has advanced to the point that such a spectacular feat is possible is a compelling reason to embrace de-extinction, not to shun it. "What intrigues me is just that it's really cool," Greely says. "A saber-toothed cat? It would be neat to see one of those."

Chinese river dolphin

Statement Evaluation

Read the passage again. Then read the following statements. Check whether each statement is True (T), False (F), or an Inference (I). If a statement is false, rewrite it so that it is true. Then go back to the passage and find the information that supports your answers.

1. _____ The Pyrenean ibex went extinct through natural causes.

_____

2. _____ The DNA of the last Pyrenean ibex was used to create another ibex.

_____

3. _____ Cloning an animal using cells from another animal is usually unsuccessful.

_____

4. _____ The de-extinction of some species will not take place for many years.

_____

5. _____ Fernández-Arias believes that species de-extinction is possible now.

_____

6. _____ Ross MacPhee is not sure that bringing back extinct species is a good idea.

_____

7. _____ A modern-day elephant may be able to give birth to a mammoth.

_____

8. _____ Scientists have been able to collect eggs from an elephant.

_____

9. _____ A female elephant's period of pregnancy is two years.

_____

10. _____ The environment that some extinct animals lived in no longer exists.

_____

Reading Analysis

Read each question carefully. Circle the letter or number of the correct answer, or write your answer in the space provided.

1. Read lines 4–5. **Drove down** means
   a. moved to another location.
   b. caused to reduce rapidly.
   c. drove away from a place.

2. Read lines 7–11.
   a. A **radio collar**
      1. provides opportunities to listen to an animal.
      2. allows scientists to know where an animal is.
      3. keeps an animal in a restricted area.
   b. **Released** means
      1. freed.
      2. followed.
      3. communicated.
   c. **Officially** means
      1. unfortunately.
      2. formally.
      3. probably.

3. Read lines 12–15.

   a. **Preserved** means
      1. recorded.
      2. studied.
      3. stored.

   b. **Injected** means
      1. copied over.
      2. forced into.
      3. taken out.

   c. **Nuclei**
      1. contain DNA.
      2. are cells.
      3. are reproductions.

   d. **Implanted** means
      1. taken.
      2. grown.
      3. inserted.

   e. A **surrogate** mother is a(n)
      1. improvement.
      2. original.
      3. substitute.

   f. A **clone** of an animal is
      1. the natural offspring of that animal.
      2. an exact copy of that animal.
      3. a related species of that animal.

4. Read lines 17–20.

   a. An **endangered** species
      1. is extinct.
      2. may be dangerous.
      3. may become extinct.

   b. These sentences mean
      1. scientists are worried that many more animals will become extinct.
      2. there is a long list of animals that have become extinct.
      3. humans have killed bucardos and made them extinct.

   c. **Reverse** means
      1. slow down.
      2. speed up.
      3. turn back.

5. Read lines 21–22.

    a. **Notion** means

        1. idea.

        2. plan.

        3. dream.

    b. **Vanished** means

        1. unknown.

        2. missing.

        3. extinct.

    c. **Hovered** means

        1. looked.

        2. balanced.

        3. waited.

    d. This sentence means that bringing extinct species back to life

        1. has been considered both possible and impossible at the same time.

        2. has always been considered completely impossible.

        3. has always been considered possible.

6. Read lines 30–32. Match each profession with its definition.

    _____ 1. conservationist   a. a person whose job is to protect plants, animals, and natural resources

    _____ 2. ethicist   b. a scientist who studies the variation of inherited characteristics

    _____ 3. geneticist   c. a scientist who studies plants and wild animals as well as their behavior and environments

    _____ 4. wildlife biologist   d. someone who studies what is morally right and wrong

7. Read line 32. **Consensus** means

    a. a serious scientific decision.

    b. an agreement among a group of people.

    c. a belief that something may be done.

8. Read lines 41–43.

  a. **Diversity** means

    1. genetics.

    2. preservation.

    3. variety.

  b. **Derived from** means

    1. taken from.

    2. changed from.

    3. protected from.

9. Read lines 44–45. This sentence means that ten years ago Fernández-Arias

  1. didn't want to bring back the bucardo.

  2. didn't know that the bucardo was extinct.

  3. didn't have the cloning technology he needed.

10. In line 55, a **viable cell** means

_____

11. Read lines 68–69.

  a. **Hurdle** means

    1. plan.

    2. idea.

    3. difficulty.

  b. **Formidable** means

    1. very frightening.

    2. difficult to overcome.

    3. extremely detailed.

12. Read lines 82–86.

  a. **Advocates** means

    1. supporters.

    2. opponents

  b. **Cutting-edge** means

    1. scientific; exact.

    2. proven; reliable.

    3. newest; innovative.

13. Read lines 91–93. **Futile** means

  a. expensive.

  b. useless.

  c. wasteful.

14. Read lines 95–96. **Resolved** means
   a. cleared up.
   b. proven.
   c. considered.

15. What is the main idea of the passage?
   a. Over time, many animals have become extinct, both from natural causes and because of humans.
   b. Many animals have become extinct, and scientists have been trying to bring them back to life.
   c. Scientists have been working on ways to bring extinct species back to life, but not everyone agrees that this is a good idea.

Vocabulary Skills

PART 1

Recognizing Word Forms

In English, there are several ways that adjectives change to nouns. Some adjectives become nouns by adding the suffix -ity, for example, *possible (adj.), possibility (n.)*.

Complete each sentence with the correct word form on the left. All the nouns are singular.

actual *(adj.)*   **1.** Some scientists question the _____ of bringing back an

actuality *(n.)*   extinct species. The de-extinction of an _____ species like

the bucardo would raise many concerns.

diverse *(adj.)*   **2.** _____ wild plant species, which are also in danger of

diversity *(n.)*   extinction, supply us with natural compounds used in medicines. We rely

on biological _____ for new pharmaceutical drugs.

real *(adj.)*   **3.** Although attempts to bring back an extinct species are a

reality *(n.)*   _____ , no one has succeeded yet. However, bringing

extinct species back to life will become a _____ possibility in

the future.

viable *(adj.)*

viability *(n.)*

4. In order to clone an extinct mammoth, a _____ cell must first be obtained. The _____ of finding such a cell is a formidable hurdle.

vulnerable *(adj.)*

vulnerability *(n.)*

5. Not only animal species, but plant species as well are _____ to extinction. Their _____ seems to increase even more due to pollution and other pressures on the environment.

PART 2

Using a Dictionary

In English, words may have more than one meaning, depending on the context. For example, *preserve* may mean to guard, or to protect from harm or change. (*The government preserves the rights of the individual person.*) It may also mean to maintain, keep in good condition. (*She preserves her health by eating sensibly and exercising.*) In addition, *preserve* can mean to prevent food from spoiling. (*Keeping food in the refrigerator preserves its freshness.*)

1. Read the following sentence. Use the context to help you understand the word in bold. Then read the dictionary entry for **divide** and circle the appropriate definition.
For thousands of years it lived high in the Pyrenees, the mountain range that **divides** France from Spain.

---

divide /dɪ'vaɪd/ *v.* **-vided, -viding, -vides** **1** [T] to separate (s.t. into shares): *Divide the candy between the two children.* **2** [I;T] to separate (into parts), break up: *They have divided the first floor into five rooms.* ‖*The huge corporation divided into smaller companies.* **3** [T] to break up, cause to disagree: *Arguments over politics divided the two brothers.* **4** [I;T] to figure how many times one number contains another: *4 divided by 2 is 2.*

---

2. Circle the letter of the sentence that has the appropriate meaning of **divide**.
a. For thousands of years it lived high in the Pyrenees, the mountain range that helps France and Spain figure how many times one number contains another.
b. For thousands of years it lived high in the Pyrenees, the mountain range that breaks up France and Spain into separate parts.
c. For thousands of years it lived high in the Pyrenees, the mountain range that separates France and Spain into shares.
d. For thousands of years it lived high in the Pyrenees, the mountain range that causes France and Spain to disagree.

3. **Divide** means
   a. separate into equal parts.
   b. create a boundary between two areas.
   c. create a disagreement between countries.

4. Read the following sentence. Use the context to help you understand the word in bold. Then read the dictionary entry for **true** and circle the appropriate definition.
   Celia's clone is the closest that anyone has gotten to **true** de-extinction.

   > **true** /tru/ *adj.* **truer, truest** **1** (*syns.*) accurate, correct. *Ant.* false.: *Reporters dig for* **true** *facts in a story, not rumors. Reporters dig for* **accurate** *facts in a story, not rumors.* **2** (*syns.*) proven, verified: *What she says is* **true** *because witnesses saw it too. What she says is* **proven** *(or)* **verified** *because witnesses saw it too.* **3** (*syns.*) faithful, loyal: *He is* **true** *to his wife and does not fool around. He is* **faithful** *to his wife and does not fool around.* **4** (*syns.*) sincere, dedicated: *Our teacher has a* **true** *interest in her students. Our teacher has a* **sincere** *interest in her students.* **5** (*syns.*) genuine, legal. *Ant.* fake.: *That safe deposit box contained a* **true** *copy of my father's will. That safe deposit box contained a* **genuine** *copy of my father's will.*

5. Circle the letter of the sentence that has the appropriate meaning of **true**.
   a. Celia's clone is the closest that anyone has gotten to sincere de-extinction.
   b. Celia's clone is the closest that anyone has gotten to correct de-extinction.
   c. Celia's clone is the closest that anyone has gotten to genuine de-extinction
   d. Celia's clone is the closest that anyone has gotten to faithful de-extinction.

6. **True** means
   a. actual.
   b. loyal.
   c. proven.

7. Read the following sentence. Use the context to help you understand the word in bold. Then read the dictionary entry for **concrete** and circle the appropriate definition.
   Other scientists who favor de-extinction argue that there will be **concrete** benefits.

   > **concrete** /kɑnˈkrit, ˈkɑŋˌkrit/ *adj.* **1** dealing with facts and certainties: *The police have concrete evidence (proof, facts) about who committed the crime.* **2** about real, specific things and situations, not general ideas: *She gave some concrete examples of how to put their new knowledge to use.* **3** made of concrete: *This is a concrete sidewalk.*

8. Circle the letter of the sentence that has the appropriate meaning of **concrete**.
   a. Other scientists who favor de-extinction argue that there will be benefits dealing with facts.
   b. Other scientists who favor de-extinction argue that there will be real benefits.
   c. Other scientists who favor de-extinction argue that there will be benefits made of concrete.

9. **Concrete** means

   a. existing.

   b. solid.

   c. actual.

Vocabulary in Context

consensus *(n.)*	drove down *(v.)*	hurdle *(n.)*	preserve *(v.)*
cutting-edge *(adj.)*	futile *(adj.)*	officially *(adv.)*	vanished *(v.)*
derive *(v.)*	hovered *(v.)*		

Read the following sentences. Complete each sentence with the correct word from the box. Use each word only once.

1. The recent construction of factories near my neighborhood _____ the value of homes in the area.

2. The child _____ between laughing and crying when she was surprised by the clown at the circus.

3. Many people feel it's important to _____ their customs and language when they move to a different country.

4. When Clara received her university diploma, she _____ became a college graduate.

5. The students couldn't decide on what movie to see together. Finally after an hour of discussion, they happily reached a(n) _____ .

6. Many patients have recently visited the new hospital in this city because of its excellent doctors and _____ technology.

7. Learning the new language was the first _____ that Felipe had to overcome when he moved to the United States.

8. Trying to teach my grandmother how to use a tablet is _____ . She refuses to learn!

9. Since Yakob doesn't _____ any pleasure from his job, he has decided to change careers.

10. Although Stella was nervous about the new school, her fears quickly _____ after she met her helpful teacher and friendly classmates.

Reading Skill

Understanding a Graphic

Graphics often accompany a reading to illustrate a difficult concept. Understanding this type of illustration increases your understanding of a reading.

Examine the following graphic. Match each statement to a letter on the graphic.

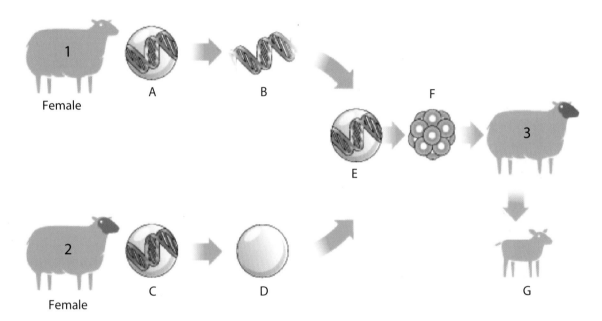

_____ The DNA from the first sheep is injected into an egg cell from the second sheep.

_____ The third sheep gives birth to a lamb, which is a clone of the first sheep.

_____ An egg cell is taken from a second female sheep.

_____ DNA is extracted from the nucleus of the female sheep's body cell.

_____ The egg cell with the first sheep's DNA is developed into an embryo and placed into the womb of a third sheep.

_____ A body cell is taken from a female sheep.

_____ The nucleus is removed from the second female sheep's egg cell.

Information Recall

Read the passage again, and review the information in the graphic. Then answer the questions.

1. Why do many scientists want to bring extinct animals back to life?

   _____

2. How close are scientists to being able to clone an extinct animal?

   _____

3. How do scientists choose an animal surrogate?
   a. They select a healthy animal that can carry a clone to term.
   b. They select a species closely related to the extinct species.
   c. They select a female of the same species as the extinct species.

4. Why is the nucleus removed from the second female sheep's egg cell?
   a. To make sure the second sheep doesn't give birth.
   b. To replace the second sheep's DNA with the first sheep's DNA.
   c. To make sure the third sheep's DNA is protected.

5. Why isn't the lamb a clone of the third sheep?
   a. Because it does not have the third sheep's DNA
   b. Because it has the second sheep's egg cell
   c. Because it has the first sheep's nucleus

6. How is it possible for a lamb to be a clone, or exact copy, of sheep number one?

   _____

   _____

Writing a Summary

When writing a summary, it is important to include only main ideas. Use your own words; do not copy from the reading.

Write a brief summary of the passage. It should not be more than five sentences. Use your own words. Be sure to indent the first sentence.

_____

_____

_____

_____

_____

_____

_____

Another Perspective

🎧 **Read the article and answer the questions that follow.**

CD 1
TR 23

Extinction: Is it really that bad?

by Euan Ritchie, *Australian Geographic*

Perhaps society's biggest challenge, and arguably our largest failure, is the continuing loss of species from Earth. We still have little idea of how many species exist on Earth. Only a fraction (somewhere around 1.5 million of an estimated 5 million) have been formally described, and even fewer assessed for their
5   conservation status. How do we conserve what we don't know exists?

Extinction Is a Natural Process

It is important to note that extinction, or the permanent loss of species, is a natural process that works in conjunction with speciation—the creation of new species through evolution.

"Normal" rates of extinction vary through time but are typically in the order of one
10   to two species per year. Current rates of extinction, however, are estimated to have reached up to 10,000 times this rate. Put bluntly, the annual species body count is no longer a mere handful, it's an avalanche.

There have been at least five episodes of mass extinctions in the past, during which anywhere from 60 to 96 percent of existing species became extinct. Indeed, 99 percent of all existing species that have ever existed are now extinct.

Volcanic eruptions and asteroid impacts are among the causes of previous mass extinctions—including the demise of the dinosaurs. Yes, mass extinctions are not unprecedented. The difference this time is that humanity is the cause of Earth's sixth mass extinction event, through human-induced impacts, such as habitat modification and climate change.

Some 875 species have been recorded as declining to extinction between 1500 and 2009, which is entirely consistent with an extinction rate of one to two species per year. What, then, are the grounds for supposing that the current rate of extinction actually exceeds this value by such a huge margin?

The key phrase is "have been recorded." As already discussed, the majority of species have not been identified or described. A reasonable supposition is that unrecognized species are lost at a rate comparable with that of known ones.

Why does extinction matter?

But why should it matter to us if we have a few less species? The simple answer is that we are connected to and deeply dependent on other species. From pollination of our crops by bees, to carbon storage by our forests, and even the bacteria in our mouths, we rely upon biodiversity for our very existence. We neglect this at our own peril.

Doom-and-gloom predictions tend to paralyze us, rather than jolting us into action. So what can be done? There are wonderful examples of individuals and organizations working at both small and large scales to tackle, and even sometimes turn back, the tide of extinctions.

But what is urgently needed, of course, is radical change in society as a whole in the way it interacts with its environment. Until then, my fellow ecologists and I must continue to work hard to spread awareness of society's biggest challenge.

A Tyrannosaurus rex skeleton greets visitors at the California Academy of Sciences.

Questions for Another Perspective

1. Why does the author say that, "the annual species body count is no longer a mere handful, it's an avalanche"?

_____

_____

2. How is the cause of Earth's sixth mass extinction event different from previous mass extinctions?

_____

_____

3. Why does it matter to us if we have fewer species?

_____

_____

4. What changes can society make to stop or reverse extinction?

_____

_____

Topics for Discussion and Writing

1. In 1989, Spanish scientists believed that only a dozen bucardos were left alive. What do you think they might have done at that time to try to save the species?

2. Why might it be worthwhile to bring back species that have recently become extinct? Why might it not be worthwhile?

3. Why might it be worthwhile to bring back species that have become extinct thousands or even millions of years ago? Why might it not be worthwhile?

4. Geneticists, wildlife biologists, conservationists, and ethicists met to discuss the possibility of de-extinction. Why might ethicists have been at the meeting?

5. Write in your journal. If you were able to bring back one species from extinction, which species would you choose? Why would you choose that species for de-extinction?

Chisels and brushes are used to unearth dinosaur bones in the Sahara Desert of Niger.

Critical Thinking

1. After the team from the Ordesa and Monte Perdido National Park put a radio collar on Celia, they released her back into the wild. Why do you think they might have done so, rather than keep her in captivity?

2. What are some ways that scientists and others might help prevent further extinctions of endangered animals?

3. What ethical issues might be connected to bringing species back from extinction? Why might some people believe that cloning and de-extinction are unethical?

4. In the second article, why does Euan Ritchie believe that saving species is essential, especially to human beings?

5. In the main reading, does Carl Zimmer express any bias in his presentation of information about de-extincting species? In other words, is he objective or subjective in describing ongoing efforts to bring extinct species back to life?

Model of a woolly mammoth at the Royal British Columbia Museum in Victoria, Canada

Crossword Puzzle

Review the words in the box below. Then read the clues on the next page. Write the words in the correct spaces in the puzzle.

advocates	endangered	hurdles	officially	reverse
clone	ethicist	implant	preserved	surrogate
consensus	formidable	notion	released	vanished
conservationists	futile	nucleus	resolved	viable
diversity	geneticist			

Crossword Puzzle Clues

ACROSS CLUES

6. The sheep Dolly was the very first successful _____ of a mammal.

7. The _____, or idea, of species de-extinction is fascinating.

8. DNA is located in the _____, in the center of a cell.

9. In the de-extinction process, scientists need to _____ eggs into a substitute mother.

12. Many problems need to be _____ before reviving a species becomes a reality.

14. Many _____ wish to see the revival of animals driven to extinction by humans.

17. Scientists need to extract _____ cells from an organism for reproduction.

18. In addition to animals, many plants have become _____ extinct, too.

19. Some animals are tagged with radio collars and then _____ back into the wild.

20. Scientists have reached a(n) _____ on the possibility of bringing back an extinct animal.

21. A(n) _____ is interested in whether something is morally right or morally wrong.

22. Saving animals in danger of extinction is a(n) _____ task! It is very hard to accomplish.

DOWN CLUES

1. We cannot _____ most extinctions. Once an organism is extinct, it is gone forever.

2. Only five white rhinoceroses remain in the world. Attempts to save this species may be _____.

3. Bringing extinct species back to life has many _____ as well as many opponents.

4. A(n) _____ studies heredity and the variation of living organisms.

5. There are many _____ to overcome before the successful de-extinction of a mammoth.

10. The bodies of mammoths have been discovered very well _____ in the cold Siberian temperatures.

11. A vast number of species have _____ from existence as a result of human action.

13. A fertilized egg needs to be inserted into a(n) _____, or foster, mother.

15. The mountain gorilla is at the top of the _____ species list and may be extinct soon.

16. Biological _____ in both animals and plants is essential to life on Earth.

CHAPTER 12

Life Beyond Earth: Almost within Reach

Enceladus ice geyser

Prereading

1. Work with a partner or in a small group. Write a definition of *life*. Then as a class, compare your definitions and create a single definition of *life*.

2. What are some ways that scientists are searching for life beyond Earth?

3. Read the title of this article. Does the author believe that we will soon find life beyond Earth? Why do you think this?

Reading

🎧 **Read the passage carefully. Then complete the exercises that follow.**

CD 1
TR 24

Life Beyond Earth: Almost within Reach

by Jenna Iacurci, *Nature World News*

Humans for the most part have always believed that we are not alone, but in recent decades scientists have been more proactive in their search for alien life, and thanks to a host of discoveries, that possibility now seems more plausible than ever. But what happens once we find life beyond Earth? Scientists and scholars at a recent
5 symposium sponsored by NASA and the Library of Congress aimed to answer that question.

The first attempt to make contact with aliens began in 1960, when astronomer Francis Drake pointed a radio telescope at two Sun-like stars located 11 light-years[1] away, hoping to pick up a sign of intelligent life. And though his SETI[2] experiment
10 went unanswered, we have learned a lot in the 50 years that have passed since then.

First off, recent research shows that even life on Earth can survive in some of the most extreme environments. For example, methane-consuming microbes[3] living in rocks on the ocean floor can withstand the deep ocean's oxygen-starved environment, while life can also be found hidden a half-mile beneath Antarctica's thick ice sheet,
15 where no sunlight has been felt for millions of years. So if organisms can withstand these conditions, what's to say they can't survive on other planets?

Scientists have also realized that liquid water—the hallmark sign for life—is not unique to our planet. Jupiter's moons Ganymede and Europa harbor large oceans beneath their icy surfaces that resemble those found on Earth. And out of Saturn's
20 many moons, a few show exciting promise for life. Titan, its largest and by far most famous moon, boasts a mysterious sea of methane (CH_4), while Enceladus is characterized by inexplicable geysers of water vapor and ice particles. What's more, just last month *Nature World News* reported that the moon Mimas may be added to the list of possibly habitable moons after a study hinted at a secret sea beneath its
25 surface.

And then there is the discovery of exoplanets, with more than 1,800 alien worlds beyond our solar system identified so far, according to the symposium. In fact, there may be one trillion planets in the Milky Way alone, one-fifth (or 22 percent) of which could be Earth-like.

---

[1] One **light-year** is equal to the distance that light travels in one year, about 5.88 trillion miles.
[2] **SETI** refers to the organization Search for Extraterrestrial Intelligence.
[3] **Microbes** are living organisms too small to be seen without a microscope.

According to famous American astronomer Carl Sagan, "The universe is a pretty big place. If it's just us, it seems like an awful waste of space." So scientists are on the hunt for life beyond Earth, and after 10,000 generations of humans, "Ours could be the first to know," said SETI astronomer Seth Shostak. The symposium was hosted by Steven J. Dick, the second annual Chair in Astrobiology at the Library of Congress.

A 'Three-Horse Race'

In a talk titled "Current Approaches to Finding Life Beyond Earth, and What Happens if We Do," Shostak talks of three possible scenarios, or "horse races," in which we could find life in the cosmos. One likelihood is that we find it close to home, in our own solar system. NASA's Curiosity Rover at this very moment is scouring Mars for signs of past or present life. Ancient soils, for instance, with cracked surfaces and containing hollows, suggest water was once present on the Red Planet.

Second, Shostak says, is that certain telescopes—like the James Webb Space Telescope to be launched in 2018—could "sniff out" gases such as methane and oxygen located in an exoplanet's atmosphere simply by observing the reflection of light. The last and final "horse" is that scientists could continue Drake's SETI work and keep one ear open for radio signals coming from other planets. Regardless of how we find alien life, Shostak is confident that it will happen sooner rather than later. "At least a half-dozen other worlds (besides Earth) that might have life are in our solar system. The chances of finding it, I think, are good, and if that happens, it'll happen in the next 20 years," he said during a hearing before the House Science and Technology Committee in May, as quoted by Discovery News.

"Time Scale Argument"

Humans are in the midst of a very technologically advanced generation, and we are making more and more progress every single day. Shostak believes scientists should take this fact into consideration while trying to make contact with otherworldly beings. We are not far off, he says, from developing artificial intelligence (AI)[4], so what's to say that other planets aren't striving to do the same, if they haven't done so already.

Known as the "time scale argument," this describes the idea that once we find extraterrestrials, they may be non-biological. Many researchers predict AI may become a reality by 2050—about a hundred years after the invention of computers, or a hundred and fifty years after the invention of radio communication. "The point is that, going from inventing radios to inventing thinking machines is very short—a few centuries at most," Shostak said in his lecture. "The dominant intelligence in the cosmos may well be non-biological."

---

[4] **Artificial intelligence (AI)** refers to the ability of a computer or other machine to perform actions that appear to require intelligent thought.

It may sound far-fetched, but in a talk titled "Alien Minds," Susan Schneider, a philosophy professor at the University of Connecticut, runs with the time scale argument, or "short window observation." She explains that once we find life beyond Earth, we may be contacting "super-intelligent" beings capable of things like "mind uploading" and "immortality." However, fellow speaker Lori Marino, a neuroscientist and current director of the Kimela Center for Animal Advocacy, is quick to point out that there is a huge gap between finding microbial life and finding intelligent life.

Philosophy of Life

If we do find life elsewhere halfway to the end of the century, whether it's biological or not, the discovery could greatly impact us from a philosophical perspective. Theologist Robin Lovin says: "We say in the traditions that come from the Bible that humanity is created in the image of God, or in more abstract terms we say that persons have a human dignity; that they share a status that requires us to treat all of them equally, and to treat them differently than the way we treat other life." "Thinking about human life against that backdrop," he added, "is something different than what science is doing when it looks at human life in relation to a biological background."

So scientists striving for proof that we are not alone must also take into consideration that their findings could impact society from a philosophical and religious standpoint. This, in turn, may dictate how they handle such a discovery. But until then, scientists continue making strides in their research, while also keeping in mind that the hunt for life is not just for bragging rights—it's also necessary for human survival.

That's why NASA has turned most of its attention to Mars in recent years. "If this species is to survive indefinitely, we need to become a multi-planet species," NASA chief Charles Bolden told attendees at the Humans to Mars Summit held in April. "We need to go to Mars, and Mars is a stepping stone to other solar systems." Plus, learning more about the Martian planet, he adds, may tell us more about Earth's past and future, and help determine whether or not life does indeed exist beyond Earth. "We prepare by continuing to question our assumptions about the nature of life and intelligence," conference host Dick concluded.

Curiosity Rover scooping samples of sand on Mars for laboratory analysis

Statement Evaluation

Read the passage again. Then read the following statements. Check whether each statement is True (T), False (F), or Not Mentioned (NM). If a statement is false, rewrite it so that it is true. Then go back to the passage and find the information that supports your answers.

1. _____ Scientists have finally discovered life beyond Earth.

_____

2. _____ Life on Earth can survive extreme environments similar to those on other planets.

_____

3. _____ Scientists have named all of the 1,800 alien worlds beyond our solar system.

_____

4. _____ NASA's Curiosity Rover has found proof that water once existed on Mars.

_____

5. _____ According to Seth Shostak, the chances of finding life within our own solar system are good.

_____

6. _____ Life may exist on planets closer to the sun than to Earth.

_____

7. _____ Artificial intelligence (AI) may be developed some time in the near future.

_____

8. _____ Alien life, if found, will surely be non-biological.

_____

9. _____ Any life found beyond Earth will be very philosophical.

_____

10. _____ Society on Earth will be strongly affected by the discovery of life beyond Earth.

_____

Reading Analysis

Read each question carefully. Circle the letter or number of the correct answer, or write your answer in the space provided.

1. Read lines 1–6.
- a. **Proactive** means
    1. energetic.
    2. interested.
    3. experienced.
- b. **Plausible** means
    1. exciting.
    2. probable.
    3. desirable.
- c. **Symposium** means
    1. party.
    2. building.
    3. conference.

2. Read lines 7–10.

    a. A **radio telescope**

        1. takes photographs of distant objects beyond Earth.

        2. detects signals from places beyond Earth.

    b. What do the letters **SETI** stand for?

    _____

3. Read lines 11–15.

    a. **Extreme** means

        1. unfamiliar.

        2. harsh.

        3. deep.

    b. What are **microbes**?

    _____

    c. This type of information is called a

    _____

    d. **Withstand** means

        1. stand up.

        2. enjoy.

        3. tolerate.

    e. An **oxygen-starved** environment

        1. is rich in oxygen.

        2. lacks oxygen.

4. Read lines 17–25.

    a. **Hallmark** refers to

        1. a possible characteristic.

        2. a favorite characteristic.

        3. a distinguishing characteristic.

    b. **Harbor** means

        1. show.

        2. conceal.

        3. offer.

    c. **Promise** means

        1. certainty.

        2. improbability.

        3. possibility.

d. These sentences mean that
   1. if there's liquid water, there is a good chance for life to exist.
   2. if there's liquid water, then life must surely exist.
   3. even if there's liquid water, life probably does not exist.

e. **Inexplicable** describes something that
   1. is easy to explain.
   2. cannot be explained.
   3. is impossible to understand.

f. **Habitable** means
   1. possible.
   2. livable.
   3. understandable.

5. Read lines 26–27.

a. An **exoplanet** is
   1. any planet within our solar system.
   2. any planet outside our solar system.

b. **Alien** means
   1. unknown to us.
   2. from another planet.
   3. not a citizen.

6. Read lines 30–31. Carl Sagan believed

a. that life most likely does exist somewhere in the universe.

b. that life probably does not exist anywhere in the universe.

7. Read lines 35–39.

a. A **three-horse race** refers to
   1. three horses in one race.
   2. three hypotheses.
   2. three places to look.

b. **The cosmos** means
   1. the universe.
   2. the liquid water.
   3. the planet Mars.

c. **Scouring** means
   1. cleaning.
   2. studying.
   3. searching.

8. Read lines 41–44.

   a. **Launched** means
      1. manufactured.
      2. designed.
      3. sent into space.

   b. The James Webb Space Telescope can detect gases by
      1. observing the way they reflect light.
      2. noticing their different colors.
      3. detecting how they smell.

9. Read lines 51–54.

   a. **Midst** means
      1. process.
      2. excitement.
      3. middle.

   b. **Progress** means
      1. technology.
      2. headway.
      3. generation.

   c. **Otherworldly beings** refers to

   _____

10. Read lines 54–58.

   a. What is **artificial intelligence**?

   _____

   b. **Striving** means
      1. hoping.
      2. attempting.
      3. thinking.

   c. **Non-biological** means
      1. not human.
      2. not living.
      3. not from Earth.

11. Read lines 62–63. **Dominant** means
   a. most important.
   b. most common.
   c. most unusual.

12. Read lines 64–66. **Far-fetched** means

    a. hard to believe.

    b. very distant.

    c. far in the future.

13. Read lines 73–79.

    a. A **theologist** is a person who

        1. studies humanity.

        2. studies traditions.

        3. studies religious beliefs.

    b. In these sentences, which word is a synonym for **backdrop**?

       _____

    c. These two words mean

        1. knowledge.

        2. experience.

        3. context.

14. Read lines 80–82.

    a. **Standpoint** means

        1. proof.

        2. religion.

        3. perspective.

    b. **Dictate** means

        1. determine.

        2. prove.

        3. question.

15. In line 88, a **stepping stone** is something that

    a. helps make progress.

    b. decides the future.

    c. answers a question.

16. What is the main idea of the passage?

    a. Scientists have been searching for life beyond Earth and have almost found it.

    b. Scientists have been looking for life beyond Earth, which will surely be at least as intelligent as human life.

    c. Scientists have been using several methods in their search for life beyond Earth and believe they will find it very soon.

Vocabulary Skills

PART 1

Recognizing Word Forms
In English, there are several ways that adjectives change to nouns. Some adjectives become nouns by deleting a final -t and adding -ce, for example, *relevant (adj.)*, *relevance (n.)*.

Complete each sentence with the correct word form on the left. All the nouns are singular.

different *(adj.)*

difference *(n.)*

1. Theologist Robin Lovin says that persons have a human dignity and share a status that requires us to treat all of them equally, and to treat them in a _____ way than the way we treat other life. There is a _____ between his standpoint and how science looks at human life.

intelligent *(adj.)*

intelligence *(n.)*

2. In 1960, when astronomer Francis Drake pointed a radio telescope at two Sun-like stars located 11 light-years away, he was hoping to pick up signs of _____ life. Today, however, humans are in the midst of a very technologically advanced generation, and Shostak believes we are not far from developing artificial _____ .

present *(adj.)*

presence *(n.)*

3. NASA's Curiosity Rover at this very moment is scouring Mars for signs of past or _____ life. Ancient soils, for instance, suggest the _____ of water on the Red Planet at some point.

confident *(adj.)*

confidence *(n.)*

4. Astronomer Seth Shostak is _____ that we will find life in the cosmos. This _____ comes from his belief that at least a half-dozen other worlds that might have life are in our solar system, so the chances of finding it are good.

dominant *(adj.)*

dominance *(n.)*

5. Our idea about the _____ of biological intelligence in the cosmos may one day be disproved. Shostak said in his lecture, "The _____ intelligence in the cosmos may well be non-biological."

PART 2

Antonyms

Antonyms are words with opposite meanings. For example, *close* and *far* are antonyms.

First, match each word with the correct meaning. Then write the antonym of the words in parentheses in the space provided. Use each word only once.

_____ 1. alien		a. advances
_____ 2. extreme		b. attempt
_____ 3. habitable		c. endure
_____ 4. inexplicable		d. energetic
_____ 5. plausible		e. foreign
_____ 6. proactive		f. headway
_____ 7. progress		g. livable
_____ 8. strides		h. mysterious
_____ 9. strive		i. reasonable
_____ 10. survive		j. severe

1. Planets and the moons of planets that have liquid water may be _____.
(*unlivable*)

2. Scientists have made great _____ in developing technology that can detect life on exoplanets. (*setbacks*)

3. It is quite _____ to suppose that life exists outside our solar system.
(*improbable*)

4. Some microscopic organisms _____ quite well even in environments where there is almost no oxygen. (*die*)

5. SETI scientists do not want to wait for extraterrestrials to contact us. They want to be _____ and send out signals to contact them. (*passive*)

6. If there is intelligent life on exoplanets, should we _____ to communicate with them? (*not try*)

7. The _____ that has been made in the past several years in developing technology is amazing. (*retreat*)

8. Hundreds of years ago, the idea of life somewhere else in the universe would have been _____. (*understandable*)

9. Extraterrestrial life will most likely be very _____ to us. It may not resemble us at all. (*familiar*)

10. If life exists beyond our planet, it may live in _____ environments that would kill a human being. (*moderate*)

Vocabulary in Context

dictates *(v.)*	midst *(n.)*	scouring *(v.)*	strives *(v.)*
far-fetched *(adj.)*	plausible *(adj.)*	standpoint *(n.)*	withstand *(v.)*
harbors *(v.)*	promise *(n.)*		

Read the following sentences. Complete each sentence with the correct word from the box. Use each word only once.

1. Pia's small boat was destroyed by the hurricane because it was too weak to _____ the high winds.

2. I woke up late and had to rush to get to class on time. In the _____ of all the commotion, I forgot to bring my books!

3. The police will arrest anyone who _____ a criminal.

4. The hallmark of a child prodigy is that she constantly _____ to be the best in her field.

5. The unusually cold weather at the end of this fall seems like a _____ for a very long, snowy winter ahead.

6. The custom in that country _____ that visitors remove their shoes when they enter a home.

7. Lena's dream of becoming a doctor isn't _____ at all. She's very gifted in science and mathematics, and does extremely well in all of her university classes, too.

8. Luciana is a staunch supporter of recycling. From her _____, most things in the home can be reused or repurposed instead of simply being thrown away.

9. When Piero lost his wedding ring at the beach, he and his wife spent hours _____ the sand until they finally found it.

10. Ilana has been studying hard and getting excellent grades. It's quite _____ that she will get a scholarship to a good university.

Reading Skill

Organizing Information in a Chart

It is important to be able to create charts. Charts can help you organize and understand information that you read.

Read the passage again. Then complete the following chart.

Life on Earth: Almost within Reach	
Attempts to make contact and to discover signs of life beyond Earth	— —NASA's Curiosity Rover is on Mars looking for signs of past or present life.
Life on Earth can survive even the most extreme environments	—Methane-consuming microbes living in rocks on the ocean floor can withstand the deep ocean's oxygen-starved environment. —
Reasons to believe life may exist beyond Earth, but within our solar system	—Liquid water—the hallmark sign for life—has been found on two of Jupiter's moons, Ganymede and Europa. — — —Mimas, another of Saturn's moons, may have a secret sea beneath its surface.
One reason to believe life may exist outside our solar system	—
Possible scenarios for finding extraterrestrial life	— —Certain telescopes, like the James Webb Space Telescope to be launched in 2018, could "sniff out" gases such as methane and oxygen located in an exoplanet's atmosphere. —

Life on Earth: Almost within Reach	
The possible nature of extraterrestrial life	— —Extraterrestrial life may be "super-intelligent" beings. —
Possible impact of discovering life beyond Earth	—Philosophically and religiously: Treat extraterrestrial life differently than the way we treat humans.

Information Recall

Review the information in the chart. Then answer the questions.

1. What discoveries on Earth have persuaded scientists that life may exist beyond Earth, even in hostile environments?

_____

_____

2. What are some indications that life may exist even within our solar system?

_____

_____

_____

3. According to Seth Shostak, what are the three scenarios in which we could find life somewhere in the universe?

_____

_____

4. How might people's philosophical and religious views influence how they respond to the discovery of extraterrestrial life?

_____

_____

Write a brief summary of the passage. It should not be more than five sentences. Use your own words. Be sure to indent the first sentence.

Another Perspective

🎧 **Read the article and answer the questions that follow.**

CD 1
TR 25

Hello? Anyone out there?

by Lea Winerman, *American Psychological Association*

Douglas Vakoch, Ph.D. is perhaps the only "director of interstellar message composition" in the world, a position he holds at the Mountain View, California-based SETI Institute. "From the outset, the idea had been that if you can build a radio telescope, [extraterrestrials] would understand our math, understand our science," he says.

5   In the early 1970s, NASA sent the "Pioneer Plaques" aboard the Pioneer spacecraft. The plaques, intended to be a message to any extraterrestrials that might find them, contained drawings of humans and pictorial symbols representing our solar system and a hydrogen atom.

But Vakoch pointed out that even if intelligent extraterrestrial beings understood,
10   for example, the chemical composition of the universe, they might have such a

radically different way of representing it that our pictograms would be completely uninterpretable.

Vakoch has brought other scientists into the SETI fold. Psychologist Donald Hoffman, Ph.D., studies visual perception and builds robotic vision systems. Vakoch asked him to write a paper on the implications of human vision research for SETI communication. "The actual [visual] content that we try to communicate [to extraterrestrials] is almost surely not going to be received in the way we intended it," Hoffman says.

Given that reality, Vakoch says the key is to think about how we could "communicate something meaningful." One idea would be to start with the most basic math. "Any civilization that can communicate should know that two plus two equals four." With that basis, we could work up to communicating more complex math.

The chance that such life exists seems to be increasing. Today, we know that most stars have planets, and that perhaps 20 percent are in a habitable temperature zone. As chances have improved, a controversy has emerged: whether or not to engage in "active SETI," or broadcast targeted messages to locations more likely to contain life, rather than just "listen" with radio telescopes. Recently, a group of 28 scientists signed a petition calling for a moratorium on active SETI until a "global consensus" was reached on whether and how to do it.

Does all of this leave Vakoch frustrated? The fact that for now we can only listen for signs of extraterrestrial life? And that after decades of listening, we haven't heard a peep? "You have to be willing to invest your time in a project with no guarantee. We could go on for hundreds or thousands of years, and not get any signal, and still not be sure that we are alone."

SETI Institute telescopes

Questions for Another Perspective

1. What did NASA scientists send out into space in the 1970s? Why?

   _____

   _____

2. What do Vakoch and others say is the problem with the objects the scientists sent into space?

   _____

   _____

3. How might this problem be addressed?

   _____

   _____

4. What is the controversy regarding the search for extraterrestrial life?

   _____

   _____

5. Why do some people oppose the active search for extraterrestrial life at this time?

   _____

   _____

Topics for Discussion and Writing

1. The astronomer Carl Sagan once said "The universe is a pretty big place. If it's just us, it seems like an awful waste of space." Do you agree with him? Why or why not?

2. If scientists finally proved the existence of intelligent life on another planet, what effect might this news have on the people of Earth? Why do you think so?

3. Some people worry that we are taking a risk by making our presence on Earth known to any beings that exist beyond Earth. Are their fears justified? Why or why not?

4. Write in your journal. Imagine you have discovered a way to communicate effectively with intelligent beings beyond Earth. Would you share this information with the world? Explain your reasons.

Critical Thinking

1. If there is intelligent life somewhere in the universe, why might intelligent beings be interested in communicating with us on Earth? Why might they not be interested in letting us know they are "out there"?

2. Charles Bolden stated, "If this species is to survive indefinitely, we need to become a multi-planet species." Why might we need to become a species that lives on several planets?

3. Some scientists think that life beyond Earth may be non-biological, that is, artificial intelligence (AI), and far more advanced than human life. If so, what might we learn from such advanced beings?

4. Read the last paragraph of the second reading. Does Douglas Vakoch believe that extraterrestrial life exists? Explain your reasons for your answer.

5. Toward the end of the main reading, Jenna Iacurci mentions that the hunt for life is "necessary for human survival." What is her viewpoint regarding the future of life on Earth?

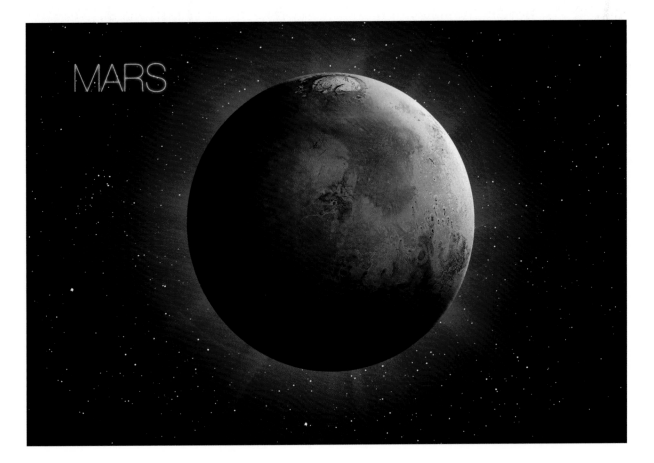

Crossword Puzzle

Review the words in the box below. Then read the clues on the next page. Write the words in the correct spaces in the puzzle.

alien	exoplanet	microbes	progress	striving
background	extreme	midst	promise	symposium
cosmos	hallmark	plausible	SETI	theologist
dictate	harbor	proactive	standpoint	withstand
dominant	launch			

Crossword Puzzle Clues

ACROSS CLUES

1. Several of Saturn's moons hold _____ for finding some signs of past or present life.

3. If life exists beyond Earth, will the _____ forms of life be biological or artificial?

4. Any planet beyond our solar system is called a(n) _____.

6. The "_____" refers to the universe.

11. The _____ of a habitable environment is the presence of liquid water.

12. Humans beings are _____ to learn more about the world we live in and the universe, too.

15. If a planet is warm enough for liquid water, it is _____ to think that life may exist there.

16. NASA plans to _____ the James Webb Space Telescope from French Guiana in 2018.

18. The conditions that exist in a given environment _____ the type of life that may exist there.

19. _____ stands for the Search for Extraterrestrial Intelligence.

20. Scientists often meet to hold a(n) _____ so they can share their ideas and research results.

21. We are in the _____ of a technological revolution. Technology is advancing faster than ever.

DOWN CLUES

1. Scientists have made great _____ in advancing our knowledge of our universe.

2. Liquid water may also _____, or shelter, life under the ice on Europa as it does on Earth.

5. The Mars Rover looks for signs of life in the form of _____, not large plants or animals.

7. From a biologist's _____, life can exist under harsh conditions, such as seas of methane.

8. A(n) _____ is an extraterrestrial.

9. A(n) _____ is interested in religious beliefs.

10. Some people do not want to wait and see if intelligent beings contact us. Some people want to be _____ and look for them.

13. Scientists look for extraterrestrial life in a biological _____, or context, but it could be artificial.

14. Human beings could not _____ the environments that exist on Jupiter or Saturn.

17. Freezing cold environments with little oxygen and no light are considered _____.

INDEX OF KEY WORDS AND PHRASES

Words with **AWL** beside them are on the Academic Word List (AWL), Coxhead (2000). The AWL is a list of the 570 highest-frequency academic word families that regularly appear in academic texts. The list was compiled by researcher Avril Coxhead from a corpus of 3.5 million words.

SKILLS INDEX

CRITICAL THINKING AND DISCUSSING

READING

TITLES

How does insight help gifted children? 87–88
A Model of Efficiency: NASA's Sustainability Base, 229–230
Parental support during childhood is key to mental and physical health
through adulthood, 20–21
The Real Secrets to a Longer Life, 130–131
Saving Her Sister's Life, 178–179
Should doctors be allowed to help terminally ill patients commit suicide? 156–157
Six Basic Principles of Using Food as Medicine, 202–204

VISUAL LITERACY
Completing:
chain of events, 107–108
charts, 38–39, 48, 85–86, 116, 140, 271–272
charts using headings, 128–129
graphic organizers, 140, 154
outlines from headings, 61–63
Creating:
Venn diagrams, 90
Crossword puzzles, 24–25, 46–47, 70–71, 92–93, 114–115, 136–137, 160–161, 184–185,
208–209, 234–235, 256–257, 278–279
Understanding:
charts and graphs, 133–135, 174–177, 226–227
diagrams, 181
graphics, 181, 249
maps, 134–135
tables, 17–18
Venn diagrams, 90

VOCABULARY, GRAMMAR, AND USAGE
Dictionary use: 197–199, 246–248
Recognizing word forms:
adjective becomes noun by deleting final –t and adding –ce, 268
noun and verb forms, same, 150–151, 171–172, 195–196
suffix -al, 82–83
suffixes -ance and -ence, 104
suffixes -ion or -tion, 125, 222
suffix -ity, 245–246
suffix -ment, 14, 36
suffix -ness, 58
Understanding:
antonyms, 172–173, 269–270
content-specific vocabulary, 15–16, 59–60, 105–106, 223–224
vocabulary in context, 16, 38, 60–61, 84–85, 106, 127, 153, 173–174, 199, 225, 248, 270
phrasal verbs, 83–84, 151–152
synonyms, 37, 126

WRITING
Journal writing, 22, 44, 68, 90, 112, 133, 159, 182, 206, 233, 254, 276
Recalling supplementary information, 21, 43, 67, 89, 111–112, 132, 158, 180, 205, 231, 253, 275
Topics for writing, 22, 44, 68, 90, 112, 132–135, 158–159, 181, 206, 232–233, 254, 275
Writing a summary, 19, 40, 64, 87, 109, 130, 155–156, 177, 202, 228, 250–251, 273

CREDITS

Text

5 "Helicopter Parenting" Hysteria: Is it as widespread as we think?" adapted from *The Myth of the Spoiled Child* by Alfie Kohn: Boston: *Da Capo,* 2014, **20 "Parental Support During Childhood Is Key to Mental and Physical Health through Adulthood"** by Benjamin A. Shaw: *American Psychological Association,* **27 "Retirement home meets day care at Providence Mount St. Vincent"** adapted from "Retirement home meets day care at Providence Mount St. Vincent," by Sami Edge: *The Seattle Times,* June 26, 2015, **41 "College Students Are Living Rent-Free in a Cleveland Retirement Home"** adapted from "College Students are Living Rent-Free in a Cleveland Retirement Home" by Heather Hansman: *Smithsonian.com,* 2015, **49 "Tablet Computers in School: Educational or Recreational?"** adapted from "Should pupils be using tablet computers in school?" by Matthew Godfrey: *Telegraph,* 2014, **65 "Classroom Aid: Learning Scientific Concepts with iPads"** by Brian Handwerk: *National Geographic News,* **75 "Are Gifted Children Born or Made?"** by Susan Logue: *Voice of America News,* 2009, **76 "The Role of Families",** adapted from "Child Prodigies and Adult Genius: A Weak Link" by Ellen Winner: *D.K. Simonton (Ed.) Handbook of Genius,* May 30, 2014, **87 "How does insight help gifted children?"** by Brendan L. Smith: *American Psychological Institute,* **95 "Babies Switched at Birth Will Not Be Returned to Their Biological Families"** adapted from "Babies Switched at Birth Will Not Be Returned to Their Biological Family" by Sam Masters: *Independent,* November 17, 2015, **96 "Damages Awarded to Families of Girls Swapped as Babies"** by Michael Leidig: *Telegraph Media Group,* **110 "El Salvador Babies Switched at Birth, Back with Parents Three Months Later"** by Rafiael Romo and Erin McLaughlin: *CNN,* **117 "Who lives longer?"** by Patricia Skalka: *McCall's,* **130 "The Real Secrets to a Longer Life"** adapted from "The Real Secrets to a Longer Life" by Amy Novotney: *The Monitor: American Psychological Association,* 2011, **141 "Matters of Life and Death",** adapted from "Matter of Life and Death" by Dr. Francis Moore, *National Academy of Sciences,* **142 "The Lure of Assisted Dying"** adapted from "As a GP, I felt the lure of assisted dying. That's why I oppose it," by Dr. Trevor Stammers: *The Spectator,* September 9, 2015, **156 "Should doctors be allowed to help terminally ill patients commit suicide?"** by Derek Humphry and Daniel Callahan: *Health,* **163 "Organ Shortage Fuels Illicit Trade in Human Parts"** by Brian Handwerk: *National Geographic,* **178 "Saving Her Sister's Life"** adapted from "Saving her Sister's Life" by Marissa Ayala: *Teen Vogue,* 2001, **187 "Will your doctor one day prescribe food as medicine?"** by Christina Farr: *KQED Science,* **188 "The Future of Medicine is Food"** adapted from "The future of medicine is food" by Deena Shanker: *Quartz,* November 10, 2015, **202 "Six Basic Principles of Using Food as Medicine"** adapted from "6 Basic Principles of Using Food as Medicine" by Dr. James S. Gordon: *mindbodygreen.com,* August 15, 2014

Photo
Cover: Zhiliang Li/National Geographic Creative.

iii Ariel Skelley/Blend Images/Getty Images, **iv** Ariel Skelley/Brand X Pictures/Getty Images, **v** Stephanie Sinclair/National Geographic Creative, **vi** Jean_de_heeckeren/RooM/Getty Images, **2–3** Ariel Skelley/Blend Images/Getty Images, **4** (tl) Roberto Westbrook/Blend Images/Getty Images, (tr) Wavebreakmedia/Shutterstock.com, **7** Vicki Beaver/Alamy Stock Photo, **13** Gary Burchell/Taxi/Getty Images, **21** Jose Luis Pelaez/Photographer's Choice/Getty images, **22** MBI/Alamy Stock Photo, **23** Terry Vine/Blend Images/Brand X Pictures/Getty Images, **26** © Erika

NOTES